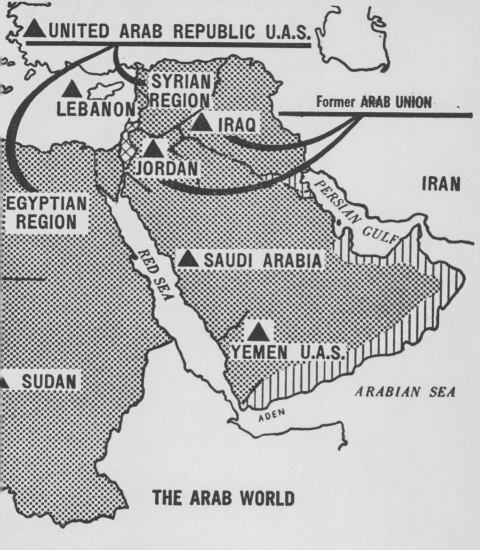

UNITED ARAB REPUBLIC U.A.S.

SYRIAN
REGION

LEBANON

IRAQ

JORDAN

Former **ARAB UNION**

IRAN

EGYPTIAN
REGION

RED SEA

SAUDI ARABIA

PERSIAN GULF

YEMEN U.A.S.

SUDAN

ARABIAN SEA

ADEN

THE ARAB WORLD

:::::::: **ARAB STATES**

▲ **ARAB LEAGUE MEMBERS**

D1572168

···KINGS AND CAMELS

Kings

Grant C. Butler

and Camels

An American in Saudi Arabia

THE DEVIN-ADAIR COMPANY   *New York*

960

The names used in this book are actual, with the exception
of a few oil-industry personnel, whose names have been fic-
tionized for obvious reasons.

To SAMI HUSSEIN, *whose love of America and things American inspired the writing of this book.*

About This Book

Grant C. Butler has made a valuable contribution to our knowledge of the Middle East in dealing with the people themselves. This readable book makes Middle Eastern people come to life. It increases the area of human understanding so essential to peace and stability in the world.

HON. HAROLD B. MINOR
President, American Friends of the Middle East
Former U.S. Ambassador to
Lebanon

Kings and Camels is an example of the superior reporting which can illuminate the most difficult political and social problems. It is exciting, lucid and perceptive. This book provides a badly needed balance in necessary information about the Arab Middle East. . . .

ROBERT R. KIRSCH
Literary Editor,
Los Angeles Times

Foreword by General Maxwell

(Major General Russell L. Maxwell headed the first American Military Mission to the Middle East during World War II. He was the first Commander of United States Army Forces in that area, with headquarters in Cairo. He later became Assistant Chief of Staff, G-4, under Generals Marshall and Eisenhower. He holds the DSM and Legion of Honor among other decorations.)

I met the author of this book for the first time in the spring of 1943, shortly after my return from the Middle East. He was a young second lieutenant fresh out of Officer Candidate School and fired with that enthusiasm for his first assignment which usually marks the OCS graduate.

For a commandant of a camp training more than 30,000 men to remember the work of one second lieutenant in the public relations department is perhaps in itself a compliment to the man. But Grant Butler made an impression. He was intensely interested in his radio work and developed a series of recruiting programs which brought credit to our camp and the Army itself.

It was during the period before he left for Europe to join the Ninth Air Force that he became interested in the Middle East, probably because I told him briefly about some of my experiences there. Little did I expect to find him fifteen years later devoting almost his entire time and effort to writing and lecturing on the Arab world.

I have watched his career with more than passing interest since he left me in 1946. He had served me in a position equivalent to aide-de-camp in Washington after his return from Germany. When he went to Saudi Arabia in 1948 with Aramco I knew that his interest in the Arab world was heightening. His letters began to reflect deep concern over many of the problems which have since faced our policymakers in Washington.

Several years ago I drove to Twenty Nine Palms, California, a desert community about 150 miles from Los Angeles, to hear Grant Butler give a lecture on Saudi Arabia. It was a hot day, and I did not look forward to sitting in a woman's club for an hour or more, even if my former aide was the speaker. But it was the only opportunity I would have that season to hear him.

The reaction to the lecture that afternoon was amazing. Perhaps it was more of a reaction to the sincerity, the warmth, the appeal of the lecturer, but the sustained applause of the hundred or more women packed into that clubhouse was striking evidence that Americans wanted to know the facts about the Arabs, that they were tired of half truths and propaganda and welcomed an objective, clear and simple report on Saudi Arabia.

I remember his display of Arab dolls, depicting costumes of the Middle East. The dolls had been made by Arab refugee women, and he used them to stimulate interest in the refugee problem. It would be difficult to guess how much money was donated to organizations aiding the Arab refugees as a result of his lectures, but I know of several organizations which gained many members as a result of his more than 1,000 lectures on the Arab world.

The clarity and sincerity which marked his articles in the *Los Angeles Times, Christian Science Monitor* and other publications was doubly apparent on the lecture platform, and I believe it is carried through in this book.

Kings and Camels is a straightforward account of how an American went to work in Saudi Arabia and came home to America to realize how little the average American appreciated the strategic importance of the area and, more important, how little he understood the people in the area. The book's emphasis is upon the cultivation of understanding between the American and Arab peoples. It points out how vital such understanding is to Saudi Arabia, to the Arabs themselves, and to Americans.

This book deals with the major issues in the Arab world, but its basic approach is to encourage some enlightened, sympathetic interest in the Arabs as people, with the idea that this kind of understanding can become most effective in molding realistic policy at the political level.

Grant Butler presents his material in the form of an informal account of his personal experiences in the Middle East, both while he lived there, working for an American oil company, and as a successful lecturer and writer who has returned to the area often. He focuses upon human interest rather than issues.

Fortunately more and more people today are realizing that a discussion of the Arab refugee problem, the state of Israel, Zionism, Arab nationalism, and communism does not have to be carried on with the threat of anti-Semitism hanging over the head of anyone who dares to criticize Israel or to reflect a point of view which is friendly to the Arab and his cause.

Americans believe in fair play, and fair play does not constitute continual presentation of one point of view to the exclusion of others. Therefore, *Kings and Camels* to me seems a timely and informative book, an honest, interesting and sometimes fascinating account of one American's look at the Arabs. It is above all else an expression of hope for a mutually rewarding friendship between peoples who have, as the author shows, a great deal in common.

RUSSELL L. MAXWELL
Major General U.S. Army
(Retired)

Washington, D.C.
June 16, 1959

♔ ... Contents

🐫 • • • KINGS AND CAMELS

🐪 ... *1*

An Arab Named Sami Hussein

I had returned from another trip to the Middle East in the summer of 1959 when I finally decided to write this book. The decision was not made without considerable soul searching. I knew that any book which reflected a point of view friendly to the Arabs was bound to encounter difficulties. It would provoke bitter retaliation from those who wished to portray the Arabs as a backward and fanatical people.

Several years before, I had talked with the vice-president of a large publishing firm in New York. He had seen my outline of the proposed book, read several chapters, and was quite enthusiastic about it. "There's only one thing," he had added. "You'd have to eliminate that chapter on the Arab refugees and leave out any discussion of Zionism. We couldn't take a chance on a boycott of our other books."

This attitude had been surprising to me, and yet I remembered what Bertha Vester had told me. This remarkable woman in her eighties runs the American Colony Hospital in Jerusalem. She could not forget the prominent New York publisher who had deleted the chapter on the Arab refugees from her book after promising to leave it intact. When she published the book herself in England with the refugee chapter included, copies disappeared from the book stores as quickly as they were supplied.

The many reasons for my not writing the book were secondary to the thought uppermost in my mind. What would my employer think of the project? I raised the subject one afternoon with the chairman of the board of Associated Piping and Engineering Company, George Humiston, who had hired me as his director of public relations.

"There's a publisher in New York," I told him, "who has expressed interest in my book on Saudi Arabia. You have given me freedom to continue my lecture work, but I do not wish to take advantage of your generosity by writing a book which might make some people angry."

"Will it be the truth?" he asked me.

"It will be as I see it," I replied. "It will be an account of my work in Saudi Arabia and the lectures which followed. I intend to discuss the Arab refugee problem and Zionism, both controversial issues."

He sat there in his office for a moment before replying. "I founded this business thirty years ago on faith in the American free enterprise system," he said. "I have never lost faith in this country or its people. I believe that understanding the people and problems of the Middle East is vital to America. I see no reason why you shouldn't write a book that helps Americans to understand the Arab point of view."

Such an attitude was completely refreshing, especially after my experiences of the past few years with people who would be expected to have some knowledge of the Arab world. There had been the vice-president of a large western oil company who had said to me at a dinner party, "Have you ever known an intelligent, educated Saudi Arab?"

There had been the public relations representative of one of the country's leading manufacturers who had said quite seriously to me, "Did you ever have slaves working for you in Saudi Arabia?"

I thought of the American Zionist publication I had read and the observations of an American minister who had lived in Saudi Arabia. He wrote about "Aramco management's continued reluctance to defend our religious rights." He went on to say "how good it would be . . . to find Americans in responsible positions abroad who cared . . . about their religious heritage."

Perhaps the real significance of that minister's article was emphasized in his further allegation: "Of course, one does not expect too much in an American oil-camp abroad. Strange characters are always drawn to such ventures. . . ."

I thought of this article and of books I had read on Saudi Arabia and the Arab world in general, books slanted or prejudiced in their treatment of the Arab, of Aramco, of Americans abroad. Could I in some small way present the truth as I saw it, as I had tried to do in my lectures throughout the country? Would this help to counteract much of the propaganda directed against Aramco and the Arabs?

Would a discussion of Islam, the religion of the Arab, help Americans to understand why the Arabs could never enter the fold of Soviet communism unless we drove them into it by our ignorance or hostility? A verse from the Arab bible, the Koran, would clarify this point: "Who is more wicked than he who prohibits God's name from being remembered in His houses of worship and he who hastens to destroy them?"

What do Saudi Arabs think of President Nasser of the United Arab Republic, and is he really a demagogue or tool of the Soviets as some would have us believe in America? And why do Arabs who once looked up to us as friends now believe we have abandoned them? These were questions that demanded answers.

I remembered, too, what the present king of Saudi Arabia had told an official of the Arabian American Oil Company in 1953 when he took control of his country: "My father's reign may be famous for its conquest and cohesion of my country. My reign will be remembered for what I do for my people."

How could I equate this statement with the oft-repeated charges that the Saud family maintains fleets of Cadillacs, luxurious palaces, and numerous harems, all at the expense of inhabitants of the desert kingdom? Could I explain this waste and also show that there has been impressive progress under the economy-minded management of Crown Prince Faisal, younger brother of King Saud?

Would the average reader be interested in the progressive measures taken to aid the people, the strengthening of the Saudi riyal, now covered 65 percent in foreign exchange or gold, the building of schools, houses, hospitals, and roads by the government? Would he understand this statement of a Saudi Arab businessman: "Within a few years you will see tremendous change here. We will take our place alongside the most progressive Arab countries." This man a few years before had been a Bedouin on the desert; he began to work for Aramco, gained an education, and now owns a contracting business.

Would the role of Aramco in Saudi Arabia be interesting for the average reader? Would he appreciate the background to a statement made by the former Aramco board chairman, Fred A. Davies, before a Senate committee in Washington: "We are pretty proud of our company. We think we have done a good job for Saudi Arabia . . . and for the United States."

When Mr. Davies points out that the United States Government has encouraged private American capital to go abroad for two reasons: to improve the standard of living and welfare of people abroad; and, as a result, to build up markets for American goods, will the average reader be interested in learning how these two objectives have been met?

Would the influence of Aramco in Saudi Arabia in the field of education be of interest? Would the operation of three company training centers where Saudi Arabs are given courses in reading and writing in English and Arabic, arithmetic and general science answer some of the questions posed by critics of Aramco? With almost half of the entire Saudi Arabian work force of 12,000 enrolled in the Aramco educational program, would the average reader want to know how this came about, and why?

There was a wealth of material about Aramco and its operations. That I knew. But I wanted to write a book that dealt with the people, their feelings and desires. I wanted Americans to understand what the young Saudi Arab said to me who had worked for Aramco for twelve years, then opened his own service station: "Like many of my people, I was suspicious of the Americans when I first went to work. Now I realize why our government and our people must work together with the Americans in a spirit of understanding and cooperation. It is the only way for our country to advance."

Aramco's part in Saudi Arabia was only part of the story I wanted to tell. What happened when I returned to America to work and live, the reaction to my articles and lectures on Saudi Arabia, was another important part of the story. My interviews with King Hussein of Jordan and King Saud, with Nuri es Said and King Faisal of Iraq, with President Nasser and other Arab leaders provided important background material for my book.

Perhaps I realized this most vividly in an illuminating moment one afternoon as I walked down Massachusetts Avenue in Washington, D.C. In the distance, I heard the familiar call of the muezzin to prayer, and saw the stone heights of the minaret. It was a call I had heard many times before in the Arab world: *"Allah akbar. . . . Ashadu an la ilaha illa Allah. . . ."* ("I testify there is no god but God.")

I might have been in Jiddah or Damascus or Beirut or Baghdad; but this call to prayer was being broadcast over the roar of traffic in Washington. The magnificent Islamic Center I saw in front of me, a place of learning and worship, had been built here by twelve nations of the Near and Middle East.

Just like the mosques I had seen in the land of Islam, halfway around the world, this one faces Mecca, famous holy city of the Moslem in Saudi Arabia. Here, not far from the White House, hand-loomed Persian rugs, ivory-inlaid wood, Turkish tile, and pink Egyptian marble surround those who come to worship or to study the teachings of the Prophet Mohammed.

"Hayya 'ala's-sala. . . . Hayya 'ala 'l-falah. . . ." ("Come to prayer. . . . Come to prosperity. . . .") called the muezzin; and though there was no interruption in the steady

rush of traffic in the street, I found myself stepping to one side of the busy sidewalk to pause for a moment, remembering. I remembered the desert of Arabia, the Bedouin kneeling on the hot sand, facing Mecca and reciting verses from the Koran.

Many things flashed across my mind that afternoon: Port Said shortly after the invasion of Egypt . . . dead Egyptians piled row on row in the hastily prepared morgues and hospitals . . . the Palestinian refugees living in their camps, existing on the seven cents a day given them by the United Nations.

I thought of visits to the palaces of kings and the tents of nomad tribesmen, harsh and sunscorched wastelands and resortlike American communities in that land of sharp contrasts, birthplace of three great religions of the world —Islam, Judaism, and Christianity.

As I walked on down the Washington street that afternoon, I knew that the problems of the Middle East would be solved, had to be solved. For there can be no peace in the world without peace in the land of Moses and Jesus and Mohammed.

Sami Hussein's words to me in Dhahran echoed in my ears: "The peace we want so badly will come when men learn to live by the words of your Bible, when we all recognize that we are 'members one of another.' "

A week later, back home in Pacific Palisades, California, I began to write this book. I had first become interested in the Middle East when I served under General Maxwell during World War II. He had piqued my interest with stories of Egypt and the Arabs of the Middle East. I remembered this vaguely the day I received a telephone call which was to change my life.

The call came from Edward W. Cochrane. As supervising sports editor of the Hearst newspapers, Ed had hired me as a young cub reporter on the Chicago *Herald-American* before World War II. We had kept in touch since his retirement to California. Now he had a proposition for me.

"Grant," he began, in his usual authoritative tone, "how would you like to go to Saudi Arabia?"

There was a blank silence at my end of the phone.

"I know a fellow," Cochrane continued, "who is hiring people in Los Angeles for the Arabian American Oil Company. He wants a young man with newspaper background and public relations experience. Are you interested?"

I had visions of Arabian horsemen galloping across the desert, turbaned shaikhs, and beautiful veiled women. Arabia. Dangerous, romantic, remote. In a word, mysterious.

Yes, I was interested. I would keep the appointment Ed Cochrane set up for me next day at the company's personnel office in Los Angeles.

Talking to the likable, athletic-looking former professional football player, Dick Richards, who was personnel manager, I began to have my doubts. This wouldn't be exactly a public relations job, he told me. I would be what they called a recreation specialist.

"You'd be assigned to Ras Tanura," he said. "Nice place. One of the company communities in Arabia, on the shores of the Persian Gulf. Wonderful sandy beach. You would be in charge of the clubhouse and the recreational facilities. Later on, of course, you could look into public relations opportunities at Dhahran, about thirty miles from there."

As for the pay, it was a fraction of what I had been making in Hollywood. Even after Richards had pointed out the real, proportionate differences in salaries and mentioned the paid vacations, I still hesitated. After all, wouldn't it amount to a detour from my chosen line of work, an interruption of the career in which I had just begun to make good?

What finally cinched my decision to take the job had nothing to do with all these practical pros and cons. It was those exciting visions of Bedouin chieftains on horseback, swords drawn, thundering down the endless stretches of swirling sand dunes—the exotic Middle East, land of mystery; that was what lured me, as I filled out the necessary applications for the job in Saudi Arabia.

My roommate, J. Robert Dube, was incredulous when I told him. "Where *is* Saudi Arabia?" he demanded. "For that matter, *what* is it?"

I laughed. "That's what I intend to find out!"

I began finding out when I was assigned, along with thirteen other men, to the first class of the training school which Aramco maintained for three years on Long Island, New York. We were to study Arabic for six weeks before leaving for the Middle East. There I met a very personable, good-looking young Saudi Arab whom Aramco had recently sent to this country as a language instructor. I knew him as Sami Hussein.

Impressed by Sami's social poise and excellent command of English, I mistakenly assumed that he must have been born and raised in some more civilized (which to me meant Westernized) part of the world. Smiling, he informed me that he had been a Bedouin on the desert, tending his camels and sheep, until, at the age of twelve, he had gone to work as a waiter in one of the American dining halls maintained by Aramco. Tactfully, he made it clear that his natural dignity and intelligence did not mark him as an exception to the rule. On the contrary, I eventually learned, the characteristics I admired in Sami were typical of the Bedouin whom I had erroneously pictured as some sort of glamorous savage who lived only to shed the blood of the infidel and abduct women of rival tribes for his own harem!

I could laugh at my erstwhile naïveté now. But I could no longer view the consequences of such naïveté, widespread in America, as a laughing matter. For now I saw that some enlightened, realistic understanding of the people of the Middle East was going to be of vital importance in the solution of the serious problems troubling their part of the world and ours. . . .

During those early days at Riverhead, living in barracks at a former United States air base to simulate the conditions of that time in Saudi Arabia, I learned to admire Sami Hussein. I also understood better my own fellow Americans who displayed as much ignorance of the Middle East as I did. A group of us would get together at night and discuss what we had learned in the classroom, our few halting words of Arabic, our obviously distorted opinions of the Arab world.

One night a member of our group asked Sami with tongue in cheek: "Isn't it true, Sami, that the Arabs have a reputation for stealing? I knew a fellow who was in North Africa during the war, and he said the Arabs took everything in sight."

Sami thought for a moment before answering; then his face lighted up with his usual smile. "Yes, there are some Arabs who steal, just as I imagine there are some Americans who steal. But in Saudi Arabia last year we had an average of forty-four people in jail out of a population of seven million."

We were amazed by the comparison between this infinitesimal figure and our own staggering crime rate, which costs Americans approximately twenty-five billion dollars a year. The Saudi method of dealing with crime, chopping off a hand for stealing, a head for murder, doubtless had much to do with this lowered crime rate.

"I can understand that you may have heard some criticism of the Arabs," Sami told us. "We're usually backward, surrounded by lots of women, and we seldom bathe. But let me tell you about an American I knew in Saudi Arabia. He was rather disliked, but he could never understand why. On his first vacation to Beirut, he asked an old Arab what kind of people lived in that city. The Arab replied with a question: 'What sort of people lived in the part of Saudi Arabia you have just come from?'

" 'Oh, a poor lot,' the American said; 'dishonest, dirty and disagreeable.'

" 'Then,' said the old Arab, 'you'll find the same sort of people here.' "

Sami had made his point, and we remembered it long after the school had ended. We also remembered Sami's thoughtful answers to our questions about the Arab world: Why had there been little or no change in Arab culture for centuries? Why did the people seem suspicious of outsiders?

"You must realize," Sami told us, "that every country seems to imagine that it is more or less the center of the world, and everyone else is on the fringe. You believe that your way of living is the only way, and my way, for example, is either a bad way or some kind of backward way. Actually, there are many things I like about your way of life, many that I like about mine. And as you live in the Arab world you will learn why we live as we do, why many Arab countries have remained backward."

The truth of Sami's statements was to be brought home to most of us in the years ahead. We were to find that the Arabs did recognize American technical and industrial superiority, that they admired our health and educational programs, appreciated our progress in scientific and technological fields, but still had definite reservations about the social and cultural aspects of our life.

"In my country," Sami had told us, "we do not see American movies, but unfortunately in other Arab countries some of your worst movies are shown, and they do not reflect credit upon America. Furthermore, some of the Americans who come to Saudi Arabia to work do not represent the best in your people."

How often I was to think of Sami's comment about American behavior in his country during the next two years. The reservoir of good will which had been built up for America in the Middle East by dedicated American missionaries, foreign-service people, and a few businessmen was being destroyed by the actions of a few Americans who thought more of a dollar bill and a bottle of whiskey than the feelings of the Arabs in whose countries they were to work and live.

Fortunately the Aramco school was an excellent place to weed out those individuals who, for one reason or another, could be expected to have difficulty in adjusting to life in Saudi Arabia. One member of our first class lasted only two weeks, as it was obvious he looked down his nose at Sami Hussein and would take the same disparaging view of other Arabs if he went to their country.

Sami's background commanded the respect of those of us who took the time to know him. It had taken him only ten years to advance to the position where he could be sent to America as one of the first two Saudi Arabs to instruct Americans in his native language.

Sami learned to love America and Americans. He liked our skyscrapers, subways, hot dogs, malted milks, and baseball games. He saw the best in us and overlooked the worst. But he still remained true to his religion. Five times a day, no matter where he was, on the baseball diamond or in the classroom, at prayer time he would take his prayer rug, kneel, and face Mecca, oblivious to the occasional joking of bystanders.

This ritual was strange to me, so I once asked Sami, "What do you tell people who kid you about praying?"

With his usual engaging smile and a twinkle in his warm brown eyes he replied, "I tell them that prayer is like a river which flows before the door of one's house. He who washes in it five times a day will keep himself pure and clean."

There were many things we learned at the Aramco school that fall of 1948, but none was more important to me than the realization that an understanding of Islam was vital to an understanding of the Arab world. Islam was fundamental to the life of the Saudi Arab. But was this really so different from our own way of life in America? Hadn't the founding fathers of our country expressed the ideals of our Christian religion in the very wording, as well as the spirit, of our Constitution?

It might have seemed strange to us that the Moslem kneels five times a day to proclaim, "There is no God but Allah, and Mohammed is his Prophet." Yet how many times a day do we all handle coins engraved with our own proclamation of faith: "In God we trust"?

I was to learn from Sami Hussein that Christians and Moslems could be good friends. Only an open mind was necessary, for open-mindedness was the beginning of understanding.

♔...2

Islam, the Religion of Mohammed

During our first week at the Aramco school on Long Island, questions were asked of us to ascertain our general knowledge about the Arab world. The questions "What is Islam?" and "Who was the Prophet Mohammed?" brought forth some interesting answers.

One of our members thought that Islam was "a game of chance, similar to bridge." Another said it was "a mysterious sect founded in the South by the Ku Klux Klan." One gentleman believed it to be "an organization of American Masons who dress in strange costumes."

The Prophet Mohammed was thought to be the man

who "wrote the *Arabian Nights.*" Another said he was "an American Negro minister who was in competition with Father Divine in New York City." One of the more reasonable answers came from one of our men who said, "Mohammed had something to do with a mountain. He either went to the mountain, or it came to him."

Weird as some of these answers might seem, they reflected the general lack of knowledge among Americans about the religion of nearly four hundred million Moslems in the world, of whom seventy million were Arabs.

When one of our classmates was asked, "What does a person have to do to become a Moslem?", he gave us an answer quite in keeping with our lack of understanding of Islam. "The Moslem must kneel on the desert each day and pray to his camel," this man told us. "A friend of mine was in North Africa during the war," he continued, "and he *really* gave me the lowdown on the Arabs."

A great deal of the mystery which seems to surround the Arab world is dispelled by the true answers to these questions: Who was the Prophet Mohammed? What is Islam? And what does it take to be a Moslem?

Mohammed the Prophet, the founder of Islam, was born about 570 A.D., in an Arabian tribe that worshiped idols, and was left an orphan in his infancy. By the time he was fifteen, he was a successful camel trader. When he was twenty-five, he married a woman, Khadijah, who was fifteen years his senior. As long as she lived, he remained devoted to her.

"But I had the impression Mohammed advocated numerous wives," I remarked to Sami, during a discussion of the life of the Prophet.

Sami shook his head and smiled. "Actually, it is just as difficult—and as expensive—to support more than one wife in Saudi Arabia as it would be here. But prior to the establishment of Islam, polygamy had long been the custom among the Arabs. At that time, the ratio of men to women was highly disproportionate, as a result of the tribal wars, so the custom was more a matter of expediency than of pleasure. But in the Koran, Mohammed was very clear on this point."

Opening the sacred book to Surah IV, Verse 3, Sami read: " 'And if ye fear that ye will not deal fairly with the orphans, marry of the women, who seem good to you, two or three or four; and if ye fear that ye cannot do justice to so many, then one only. . . . Thus it is more likely that ye will not do injustice.' "

I could see that the passage seemed to advise monogamy as preferable and to limit polygamy even while permitting it. From the same Surah, Sami quoted Verse 129: "Ye will not be able to deal equally between your wives, however much ye wish to do so. . . ." In marriage, then, and in all personal relationships, the Prophet held up to his followers an ideal of justice and honor and compassion. But as he never claimed to be a saint or a divinity, he was ever tolerant of the weaknesses of his people, realizing that they were only human, like himself. Rather than make righteousness impossible, he offered realistic ideals toward which his followers could strive in their daily lives.

Many descriptions have been written of the Prophet's physical appearance, but most agree in the main details, picturing him as a man of medium build, broad-shouldered, with dark, piercing eyes and full beard, which gave his face a gentle but forceful aspect. He was forty years old and still had displayed no indication of his destiny as a religious leader when, one night, while camped on the outskirts of the city of Mecca, he was awakened by a vision of the angel Gabriel, whose glory filled his tent with radiance.

The angel said, "O Mohammed! Thou art the Prophet of the Lord, in truth, and I am Gabriel. Write the word of the Lord."

Like every prophet before him, Mohammed shied away from this vision. He couldn't believe it. How could he "write the word of the Lord"—a man who had never even learned to read?

He went to his wife, Khadijah, in great despair. She comforted him and assured him that he must indeed be a prophet.

The vision came to Mohammed again. The angel Gabriel repeated his command. "Read in the name of the Lord, who created man out of a clot of blood; read in the name of the Most High, who taught men the use of the pen, who sheds on his soul the ray of knowledge and teaches him what before he knew not."

Mohammed wrote what the angel told him to write; and these revelations were compiled into the amazing Arab bible, *al-Quran* or the Koran, "The Reading"—one hundred and fourteen chapters of incredible beauty and dignity, by a man who knew not how to read or write.

During the next ten years of his life, Mohammed led twenty-seven campaigns or battles to establish his religion of Islam in the Middle East. In one decade he abolished idolatry in Arabia; he raised the status of women; he effectively stopped the drunkenness and immorality which had disgraced the Arabs; he taught men to love honesty, compassion, and justice; he made universal brotherhood a basic principle of common law. And in initiating all these reforms, his authority was the Koran—the Word of God which had been revealed to him.

Mohammed died in 630 A.D. in Medina. On the day of his death a huge crowd assembled outside his modest home, refusing to believe that their beloved Prophet was breath-

ing his last. Then one of his closest followers came out and
stood before the crowd and said, "Lo, as for him who used
to worship Mohammed, Mohammed is dead. But as for him
who used to worship Allah, Allah still lives." And then the
follower repeated from the Koran these words: "For Mohammed is but a messenger . . . the like of whom have
passed this way before. But Allah will always remain."

What does it take to be a Moslem? There are five disci-
plines. First, the Moslem must confess daily, "There is no
God but Allah, and Mohammed is his Prophet." Wherever
you go in the Moslem world at prayer time, you will hear
it chanted in Arabic: *"La ilaha illa Allah: Mohammed
rasul Allah."*

Second, the Moslem prays five times a day: in the morning, at noon, in the afternoon, at night, and before he goes
to bed. Third, he contributes two and one-half percent of
his total income each year to charity. Fourth, he observes
for the month of Ramadhan each year a daily fast requiring
that the Moslem neither drink water nor eat food from
sunup in the morning until sundown at night. And finally,
if possible, he should once during his lifetime make a pilgrimage to the Holy City of Mecca, after which he may
call himself "hajji," a title of respect which puts him a
little above his fellowmen.

The five pillars, then, of Islam (which means submission
to the will of God) are the profession of faith, prayer, alms-
giving, fasting during the month of Ramadhan, and the
pilgrimage. Mohammed declared Friday to be the sacred
day, just as Christians had Sunday set aside for worship and
the Jews had Saturday. At first, Moslems faced Jerusalem
when they prayed. But when Mohammed found that the
Jews would not accept Islam, he named Mecca as the
Kiblah, or prayer goal, and this city became the site of the
great mosque.

Mohammed signed a treaty with the Jews providing for equal rights and full religious liberty. Even though the Jews, who contended that the Messiah must be of the house of David, refused to recognize a prophet from the house of Ishmael, Mohammed remembered their help in bringing him to Medina. Moslems today believe that Jesus taught almost the same message as Mohammed, but they reject the Trinity and believe that the Christians corrupted their scriptures by introducing the Incarnation, the Crucifixion, and the Resurrection. In the past, there have been deep and recurring differences between Moslems and Christians, as evidenced by the struggle between the caliphate and Byzantium, and the Crusades. But today, the modern Moslem still subscribes to the view expressed in the Koran, Surah II, Verse 136:

"We believe in Allah, and in what has been revealed to us, and to Abraham, and to Ishmael, and Isaac, and to Jacob and the tribes; and what was given to Moses and to Jesus and to the prophets from Allah; nor make we any distinction between them."

But while Islam thus regards both Judaism and Christianity as formally almost identical with itself, it is today still difficult to explain Islam to the Christian, for the religion of the Moslem has many aspects: the strict tradition of the orthodox (Sunni) Islam; Shiism, another major system of Islamic doctrines; Sufism, the mysticism of Islam which began with the practice of meditation on the Koran and ended with the soul's approach to God. The Shari'ah, the law of Islam, is the fundamental code of Saudi Arabia and prevails in numerous matters that in other countries would fall within the province of civil law. A *qadhi,* or judge, dispenses justice in Saudi Arabian villages in accordance with the Koran.

Yet, for the vast majority of Moslems, Islam is an ex-

tremely simple and personal religion. There are no rites
or ceremonies performed by priests. The *imam* may lead
the people in their prayers, and the *qadhi* may preside in
their courts of law; but the basic religious concept is one
of a relationship directly between the individual and
Allah without any human being acting as intercessor. The
mosques provide the Moslems with surroundings appropriate for worship, but there are no sermons or services
as in Christian churches and Jewish temples.

A Moslem of the purest faith may live and die without
ever being able to go to Mecca. But the gain is great for
one who makes the trip, whose act of religious obedience
strengthens his hope of Paradise and entitles him to the
increased respect of his fellowmen during the rest of his
life. The *hajj,* or pilgrimage, is performed in accordance
with the Koran during the months following Ramadhan.
As many as 250,000 pilgrims, arriving on foot, by camel,
ship, plane, and automobile from Africa, Indonesia, Syria,
Iraq, Pakistan, and every place in the world where Moslems live, have assembled at one time in Mecca.

When the pilgrim is ready to leave his house, he repeats
the prayer for the journey: "O God, you are my Compan-
ion on the journey, and you are the One who remains with
my people. O God, roll up the earth for us. . . ."

At a designated point on each principal route into
Mecca, the pilgrims enter into a state of purity known as
ihram. They clip their nails, shave or cut their hair, bathe,
discard headgear, and exchange shoes for sandals. They don
the *ihram* garment, which consists of two long pieces of
white seamless cloth, one wound about the waist and the
other around the shoulders. These simple garments make
all men, rich and poor, great and small, equal during the
rendering of homage to their Creator. The Moslem in
ihram is forbidden to indulge in any pleasures of the flesh,

to use perfumes, to wear garments with seams, to destroy any living plant or animal in Sacred Territory. Finally, the pilgrims enter the Holy City for the religious ceremonies, preferably on foot—as their Prophet said that every step of the man who walks is a hundred times better than the step of the mount bearing the rider.

I found it interesting to compare the Mecca ritual to such Christian ceremonies as baptism and communion. But I was also impressed by the similarities between the two religions, especially by Mohammed's recognition of the validity of the other religious systems, Judaism and Christianity. When I commented on this to my teacher, Sami, he picked up his Koran and said, "This same idea is expressed elsewhere in the Koran. Listen." And he read from Surah V, Verses 82 and 83: "Thou wilt find the most vehement of mankind in hostility to those who believe [to be] . . . the idolaters. And thou wilt find the nearest of them in affection . . . [to be] those who say: Lo! we are Christians. That is because there are among them priests and monks, and because they are not proud. When they listen to that which hath been revealed unto the messenger, thou seest their eyes overflow with tears because of their recognition of the Truth. . . . And [how should we not] hope that the Lord will bring us in along with righteous folk?"

This much information about Mohammed and Islam would be a big help for anyone planning to go to Saudi Arabia, I decided. Certainly it had opened my eyes and led me to feel that I could expect to get along socially with Moslems much more easily than I had supposed.

"Your people no longer seem so strange to me," I told Sami Hussein. "I'll probably feel right at home with them."

"I trust you will," he said, seriously. "For it is true

that our peoples do have much in common. Still you should be prepared for differences that may sometimes surprise you or alarm you. I hope, for example, that you will not be unduly shocked when you see our method of punishment. It is based upon the Koran's law: 'An eye for an eye, a tooth for a tooth.' "

When I arrived in Saudi Arabia a few weeks later, during the bus trip from the Dhahran airport I was suddenly reminded of Sami's warning. Passing the high barbed-wire fence that surrounded the American community, I noticed something hung up near the gate. It looked like a hand. . . .

I turned to the fellow seated next to me and said, "That looks like a hand up there!"

He stared for a minute at the fence, then nodded. "It is."

I learned presently that the Arabs had conducted a very graphic display of justice in front of the Arab employees a few hours before our arrival. A young Arab houseboy who had been caught stealing for the third time had been taken out in front of the community to have his hand chopped off.

The severed hand was left hanging on the fence for several days—a lesson to other employees. Some time afterward, I witnessed a beheading.

How could I reconcile such practices with what I had thus far learned of Islam? It was a good thing Sami had cautioned me to prepare myself for an occasional surprise, for otherwise all his patient effort to instruct me about his people might have gone in vain. Like many another American, I might, upon my first glimpse of an aspect which seemed barbaric to me, have decided that the entire Moslem culture was uncivilized and altogether inferior.

As it was, I felt inclined to think the matter through

before jumping to any unwarranted conclusions. I reflected
that in the United States we shot our murderers, electro-
cuted them, hanged them, or put them in gas chambers;
each of these methods killed the condemned man just as
dead as the sword-and-dagger execution of the Arabs. On
the other hand, in our courts, which we considered as humane as we knew how to make them, judges and juries
were kept busy the year around trying the increasingly
heavy load of criminal cases; while here in the villages and
on the desert of Saudi Arabia, where justice was dispensed
by the local *qadhi* in accordance with Koranic law, there
were amazingly few thieves and murderers to be dealt with
at any time.

The low crime rate might be ascribed at least partly, I
thought, to the effectiveness of these special forms of punishment. But since law enforcement was handled differently
in other predominantly Moslem countries, such as Syria,
Egypt, and Iraq, it seemed reasonable to suppose that some
other cultural feature shared in common might account for
the phenomenon. Again, the teachings of the Koran seemed
to provide some of the answers.

For I was learning, by now, that while Islam was different things to different people, every devout Moslem appeared to know the value of prayer and to regard it as more
important to himself than his material possessions. Prayer
was his source of comfort and inspiration; it was the basis
of his hospitality, his friendliness, his willingness to offer
anything he might have in his home or his tent to the
stranger in need.

A tall, vividly handsome Bedouin leader, whom I met
at one of the oil-company outposts on the desert, told me
about seeing an American movie that had been shown
there for the employees and their guests. Part of the action
had been filmed near a modern dam on one of the great

rivers. My Bedouin acquaintance had been fascinated by
the way the boats would enter the locks, and the gates then
close behind and open above so that water could enter,
filling the closed lock until the boats gradually rose to the
next level, where they could continue their journey.

"I think of that magnificent dam," he said, a smile soften-
ing his dark features, "when you ask me what prayer means
to me. Sometimes we go along on our own power, finding
enough food and water and possessions. But then we come
to a place where we need outside help to move us along the
stream of life. This help is prayer, the power of Islam."

There was no question in this Bedouin's mind that such
power was available to everyone, for it came from the one,
the only, supreme being, Allah. Without the help of Allah,
he said, we cannot go on in life for any length of time.
Without it we cannot lock out discouragement and rise
above unfavorable circumstance.

Another time, I asked my Arab driver how he could
endure the fast of Ramadhan for one entire month—the
ninth month of the Moslem year, when temperatures
often ranged daily from 90 to 130 degrees.

My driver spoke very little English, but his reply was
eloquent in its simplicity: "Through my fasting, I come to
know Allah better. I know my brother better. . . . Even
my American brother."

I was beginning to realize that in every devout Moslem,
from the most humble to the most important and powerful
leaders, was this same feeling of personal closeness to his
benevolent and protective Allah. Only among the more
sophisticated and "modern-minded" Arabs of the large
cities did I encounter an indifference to prayer—which was
often accompanied, I thought, by a corresponding lack of
confidence and contentment.

On Christmas night, my first year in Saudi Arabia, I received the most impressive indications of the possibilities for unity between the Moslem viewpoint and the Christian. I was living in Ras Tanura on the shores of the Persian Gulf, about 10,000 miles away from the people I knew. I had been invited to a dinner party by an American family whom I had recently met. There were to be some Arab guests, several diplomats, and a few bachelors like myself.

I had walked up the beach late that afternoon toward the American settlement, feeling very lonely. I was early, so I sat on the beach, watching the sun set into the desert sands. It was unbelievably quiet. Flares from the oil fields miles away cast their dull red glow in the sky. The desert stretched endlessly away from the calm waters in front of me. I watched a camel caravan on the crest of a dune far down the coast, moving gracefully into the dusk. Somehow it didn't seem like Christmas Eve; and yet here I was in a land where two thousand years ago the greatest man who had ever lived had been born. . . .

Later that evening, as sixteen of us gathered in the comfortable living room of the American home after a wonderful dinner, I had to laugh at myself while confessing my moment of homesickness on the beach.

"Paradoxical, isn't it?" I observed. "What I really missed most of all was the familiar glitter and tinsel of the Christmas tree. Yet here I was sitting beneath the same desert skies where the most important event in history took place —the advent of the star of Bethlehem—which we commemorate with our Christmas tree lights! I suppose a person becomes so accustomed to the lights of the yearly celebration, he's apt to forget there ever was an original model."

My host nodded. "It's true that anyone who happened to be on that beach where you were strolling, or for that matter on this hill where our house now stands, would have seen the Christmas star in all its glory, just as the shepherds with their flocks and the three wise men saw it, shining in the East on that night two thousand years ago. Somehow that thought makes the old story of the first Christmas more meaningful to me tonight."

"It is understandable," said one respected Saudi Arabian official, "that you should feel homesick on an occasion which you are used to observing in familiar surroundings among your loved ones. But the true meaning of your faith is with you at all times, wherever you go. As it is with all of us. We Moslems are not different from you Christians in that respect."

"I am beginning to realize that more and more," I replied. "Just what would you say is the true meaning of your faith to you?"

"To me, Islam means peace, not submission," he said. "I am unorthodox in my interpretation of Islam, but I believe there are many others who feel as I do."

The Indian nurse who was present nodded her head. "Everyone who accepts peace is a Moslem," she said. "The essence of Islam is peace—peace within oneself."

The Lebanese spoke up. "You should ask her what she believes about marriage," he said with a smile.

She laughed. "Yes, I've noticed that that question is usually of special interest to Americans when a Moslem woman discusses her religious views. Well, most of us believe that our Prophet intended men to have only one wife. It seems clear from reading the Koran that he believed in monogamy, though he tolerated the polygamy of the times."

"Whatever the status of women in the Moslem world today," the Lebanese continued, "it is the result of other cultures—the Ottoman Empire, the Persian Empire— which influenced Moslems. Islam is simple and must be practiced as written. The Koran does not recognize any difference in status for men and women except as the social order dictates."

I knew that in her work at the Arab hospital the nurse often had as patients women brought in from the nomad tribes of the desert. I asked her, "What would the average Bedouin's wife say about Islam?"

"She would say that her religion is to her as is her husband, something she holds dear. She would say that the daily prayers are a source of comfort and inspiration, that a belief in a supreme being is something vital in her life, something to turn to in times of trouble."

A middle-aged Egyptian businessman, who had just come ashore from a boat moored at the Ras Tanura pier on his first visit to Saudi Arabia, shook his head. "I realize I represent a minority," he admitted, "when I say that I do not believe in any religion. I am not convinced there is a supreme being. I do think there is a governing force of some kind in the world, but I believe in natural phenomena, not spiritual phenomena. There are probably only a handful in the Middle East who believe as I do."

An Iraqi who worked for an oil company and was there on a mission for his government was soft-spoken, polite, and hesitant to discuss the subject. "Islam is the purity of the soul. It is devoid of mysticism to me. It is a system built on morality and reality. Everyone is born a Moslem, no matter what he may call himself later. I say this because every man is born free and equal, which is what Islam teaches. The essence of Islam is goodness. Man is essentially good. Every child is a reflection of the supreme being until he later learns to hate or distrust or envy. At first, the child knows only love and affection. Islam is my life. It cannot be explained in scientific terms. It can only be accepted as a vital part of one's being."

Presently, at his wife's suggestion, our host took out the
Bible and read aloud, from the Gospel of Matthew, the
story of the first Christmas. All the guests, even the Egyptian, listened with rapt attention. As we separated later I
felt that we all experienced a deepened sense of brotherhood, one with another. . . .

Much later, I found myself recalling the special quality
of that evening whenever I had occasion to discuss the
threat of communism to the Middle East. I was sure that
any devout Moslem who examined communism would find
dialectical materialism totally incompatible with his religion. But did the average Moslem realize this?

"Unfortunately, no," I was told, by Hisham Nazer, a
brilliant young Saudi Arab from Jiddah, who had just obtained his master's degree in international law from the
University of California at Los Angeles. "Better communication of information, of ideas, is urgently needed in the
Arab world today. All Arabs should know that professed
Soviet friendship for Islam in the Middle East is a tremendous fake and that, within Russia, Islam has been persecuted as much as all the Christian religions and Judaism.
The Koranic schools have been closed there and the Moslem religious festivities have been suppressed. Moscow
radio constantly alerts its listeners to what it calls the re-
actionary character of Islam. Once advised of these facts,
the Arabs would realize that the Russians' first project, if
they ever took over the Middle East, would be the destruc-
tion of Islam."

There could be no doubt about the importance of
clearer understanding on these fundamental issues—among
the Arabs themselves, whose immediate welfare was in the
balance; but also, and just as urgently, among Americans,
who can ill afford to lose a friend, and a potentially strong,
strategically vital friend, in their stand against communism.

♟...3

Aramco, the Meeting of the Twain

On a blistering hot afternoon in September, 1933, three American geologists stepped ashore from their launch at Jubail, Saudi Arabia, a tiny fishing village on the Persian Gulf. They were dressed like Arabs so as not to excite suspicion among the people who had never seen Americans before. They were armed with a letter from King Ibn Saud introducing them to the local Amir or Shaikh. They wanted guides and camels and supplies. They wanted to look for a site where oil might be found.

After a day's rest they were taken by camel train to the foot of the sprawling hill known as Jebel Dhahran. They had observed this huge formation from nearby Bahrain Island and had decided it was as good a site as any to look for oil. Here they established the first American oil base in this strange country, their only neighbors a few Arabs whose tents were pitched nearby and who came to stare incredulously at "these foreigners who want something black and sticky from under the sands."

Five years later, after many disappointments, oil was discovered in sufficient quantity to make the venture successful. During those five years the Americans fought the sand and heat, with summer temperatures ranging from 100 degrees to 130. They battled the diseases of the desert— dysentery, malaria, and smallpox. They were the pioneers who prepared the way for a new outpost of American industry.

Future Aramco employees would arrive by plane, not by launch, and would find no such primitive conditions awaiting them. For though the sand and heat remained, there were now comfortable quarters and clean kitchens to provide the necessities of good health for hygiene-conscious Americans.

The group with which I set out from New York on the forty-five-hour air trip to Dhahran had enjoyed the benefit of two months' training in the language and customs of the country. It was a gray, overcast afternoon in New York when we said goodbye to our teachers, Sami Hussein and Khalifa bin Yussef, and boarded the de-luxe company plane, aptly named "The Camel." Our passports had been procured for us, accommodations had been reserved at a hotel in Lisbon, Portugal, where in those days the Aramco flights halted for an overnight stop. The tasteful green and white interior of "The Camel" included private bedrooms for the women and children. The steward and attractive stewardess had enough equipment to outfit a complete children's ward in a hospital. The food was first class. Solid luxury all the way, I reflected—quite different from the hardships endured by those three geologists who had gone ahead of us years before!

There were forty of us on this flight—Aramco employees, with their wives and children. After dinner at Gander, Newfoundland, that first night out, we had plenty of time to get acquainted while we crossed to the Azores. A number of the men I already knew, of course, from the training classes.

Mary Holloway, however, had been a newcomer to our group when she boarded the plane in New York. She was an Aramco nurse from Dhahran, returning now after taking a patient to California. She was tall and slim, with red hair and an easy, comfortable smile. How long had she been with Aramco, I asked, and did she like it?

"I wouldn't trade my job with anyone else in the world!" she said. "I've been in Arabia four years. I've met nicer people, had more fun, and seen more interesting things than most people do in a lifetime. Besides, I've saved a lot of money."

Pete Murphy, as Irish as his name, was taking his attractive brunette wife, Patty, and their four-year-old daughter, Susan, to Ras Tanura, one of the three Aramco communities in Saudi Arabia, after waiting, as was then customary, for two years, his first hitch, to get housing points. This was his second two-year contract. How would his wife like Saudi Arabia? And his daughter?

"We were all raised in a small town. Ras Tanura is no different, except it has more to offer. Wonderful sandy beach, terrific swimming. We even have a golf course, riding stable, and plenty of sports. The kids there love the climate, and the gals have plenty to keep them occupied. Where else could I save almost my entire salary each year?"

Was Mrs. Murphy afraid of settling down in a country halfway around the world? "Of course not. My family has traveled all over the world. My father was a seaman for years; two brothers are in the Navy; and my mother came from Ireland. I'm glad to get started seeing some of the places I've always wanted to see—Bombay, Paris, London, Singapore. . . ."

We were several hours out of Gander, and most of the passengers had stretched out on the seats, which could be adjusted to various reclining angles. It was quiet in the dimly lighted cabin except for the steady hum of the engines. The Aramco captain of "The Camel" walked back through the plane, a short, well-built man on whom the neat uniform looked impressive. He was in full charge of the plane, passengers, and crew for the duration of the 14,000-mile round trip. How did he like his job?

"I flew with Pan American for six years," he said. "Had plenty of service during the war. I've got about 12,000 hours altogether. There isn't another flying job that matches this one. We fly only seventeen or eighteen weeks out of the year—maybe twenty at the most. We make this round trip in about six days, then we have two weeks off. Mighty nice to be with the family."

Aramco, I learned, in its international division had six complete crews—each comprising the plane captain, first officer, navigator, radio operator, flight engineer, purser, and stewardess. Altogether Aramco had 220 people on the payroll to keep its planes flying: 60 of them in New York and 160 in Dhahran, where the company also maintained DC-3's, Convairs and smaller planes.

Pat Neely sat next to me on "The Camel," a good-looking, heavy-set man in his early thirties. He was one of the men who had attended the Aramco school with me at Riverhead, Long Island. I found that, like me, he couldn't sleep on planes. To pass the quiet night hours, we talked about our reasons for taking jobs abroad.

Neely had been a barber, waiter, electrician, and all-around handy man. Now he was coming to Arabia as a welder. "I was making three bucks an hour, with plenty of overtime, and I still couldn't save money," he told me. "My wife and I figured it out. I spend a few years, maybe five, on this job. I've got it made. We can buy a business of our own. We've always wanted a pet shop. We love dogs, cats, all kinds of animals. It would be a nice way to retire."

Did his wife work? "Sure. She holds down a job as a stenographer, at about $250 a month. Works in one of those big insurance offices. We figure the months will go fast, until she can come and join me."

We had a delicious breakfast in the Azores that morning, then on to Lisbon and a twenty-four-hour layover with comfortable rooms at the Estoril, the scenic hotel on the shores of Portugal. My roommate was Walter Cato, a bland, baggy kind of man, fiftyish, iron-gray hair, gold-rimmed glasses, heavy features. He, too, had been at River-head. He was a schoolteacher.

"I can save more money in two years in Arabia than I can teaching school in America for ten years," he told me, as we toured Lisbon that afternoon. "But that isn't the real reason I took this job." He gazed thoughtfully out the window of the taxi as we bumped along the street, then said, "Remember the Mayflower Compact—the Pilgrim's charter of liberty?"

I glanced at him in surprise. What connection could that have with his decision to work in Arabia?

"Well," he continued, "the Pilgrims were Americans who believed in the equality of all men before God. As a schoolteacher, I believe in teaching the faith of our fore-fathers to children everywhere—but more than that, I be-

lieve in expressing these ideals in our own daily lives, so
that people of different races, colors and beliefs can see
what Americans are really like."

"You're a missionary, aren't you, Walter?" I joked.

"Not really. I just believe that in my own small way I
can be important to my country by teaching school in
Saudi Arabia. Human life seems to be filled with divisions.
We are divided into nations, races, and religions. As Christians, I think we need to see what it is that divides and
what unites men and nations. Maybe in doing this we can
discover how to understand and love one another."

We left Lisbon the next morning en route to Rome,
Damascus, and finally Dhahran. It was cool and overcast
when we circled Rome. The Vatican loomed up ahead of
us, imposing, commanding. We were on the ground in
Rome for an hour, shepherded by two Italian TWA host-
esses who served us a delicious lunch of scallopini with
white frascati wine.

From Rome to Damascus I followed our course on a
map, across the Tyrrhenian Sea, over Capri, Athens and
the Dodecanese Islands. The six-hour stretch was an opportunity to talk with some of the other Riverhead "graduates."

John Martin was a husky giant of a man, about six feet
three, well over two hundred pounds. He had been a
policeman in Chicago and had taken a job in Arabia with
the security department mainly for economic reasons. With
two children in high school and three in grammar school,
he and his wife hadn't been able to make ends meet on a
policeman's salary. Being away from his family now would
be hard. But he could visit them at the end of the first year,
and later they could join him. From then on, they could
enjoy a happy home together without the financial strain
that had become such a problem.

There are two distinct species of camels, the Arabian dromedary (*below*) with a single hump, and its Bactrian cousin from Central Asia, smaller and less tame, which has twin humps. The hump enables the animal to store surplus food, in the form of fatty tissue, while the three-section stomach carries water enough to last him for two weeks in the most grudging wastes. The camel is the Arab's transportation, food, and even wearing apparel. The hair of the animal can be spun into rugs, tents and clothing. Its thick, sweet milk makes a nourishing drink. Its hide can be transformed into leather for water pouches and saddles. The camel performs its task without complaint, traveling up to one hundred miles in a day across the desert, and transporting as much as half a ton for twenty-five miles before the sun can set. The camel is more than the "ship of the desert"; to countless Arabs, it is life.

Waagenaar—Pix

(*above*) Ibn Saud (seated), the late king of Saudi Arabia, with his son Saud, the present king. (*opposite, top*) Amir Faisal, crown prince of Saudi Arabia. (*opposite, below*) The author with Bedouins on Saudi Arabian desert.

Sami Hussein with his wife and children at their home in Levittown, New York.

Barlow Curtis was the executive of our group, a Yale graduate, prominent in society circles in New York. His wife had been a wealthy debutante. They now had two children. In coming to Saudi Arabia, he seemed to be giving up a good deal more than the others. I did not think he was motivated by financial considerations, so I was particularly interested in finding out his reasons.

"Frankly," he told me, "I got fed up with New York. I was making good money, but that doesn't mean much in a crowd where everybody is always trying to get more than the other fellow and make a bigger impression, where one's personal worth is measured by the amount of wealth one displays. I just got sick of the phony social parade. So did my wife. We thought this would give us a good opportunity to enjoy a different way of life in another part of the world, raise the kids in a quiet atmosphere for a few years."

Pete Wolford, a balding widower of forty-five, had served on a Navy destroyer during the war. "We got into the Persian Gulf a couple of times," he told me. "I met a lot of Arabs, Persians, Egyptians. I always wanted to come back to the Middle East. It's fascinating. You'll find that out for yourself."

Tina Travers was one of the American wives from Dhahran. With her six-year-old daughter and eight-year-old son she was returning after her second long vacation in the States.

"I guess we were about the happiest family in America, she told me. "Frank had fifteen years' service with Texaco, and made a good living for us. We were healthy, contented. But when we talked over his offer of a job in Arabia, it was the travel opportunity that finally won us over."

We stared out the window of her private compartment as the plane began to let down over Jubail. "There it is!"

her little girl exclaimed, excitedly, as Dhahran came into view—a cluster of low one-story buildings with nothing all around but sand and desolation. It was a sight to make a man swallow twice and wish he were back in the United States. But Mrs. Travers smiled at my obvious disappointment.

"It may sound strange to you now," she said, "but we're actually eager to get back to Dhahran. We've been homesick for it." And when I shook my head dubiously, she laughed. "You'll understand after you've been there awhile."

Well, maybe she was right, I reflected.

That night we ate our first dinner in the Dhahran dining hall, a pleasant, modern, well-lighted building, where the food was excellent. In these surroundings, it was hard to realize we were actually seven thousand miles from New York. During the meal we were all embarrassed by the spectacle of two Americans, a man and his wife, who came staggering into the hall, obviously drunk, to stumble and land on the floor in an unceremonious heap. I could never forget the looks on the faces of the young Saudi Arabian waiters who helped the couple to their feet. A few hours before, I had been rather shocked by an example of their Arab justice . . . But in view of this kind of behavior among our people, I wondered what they must think of *us*.

I had a chance to observe more of the effects, usually regrettable, of alcohol on Americans in this desert climate when I went to Ras Tanura the next day. Walter Cato and I were the only Riverhead "graduates" to be assigned to this refinery community, forty miles up the Persian Gulf.

Leaving Dhahran by bus early that morning, we bumped across the edge of the desert, passing an occasional oil derrick silhouetted against the pale blue sky, now and then catching sight of a camel train in the distance. Otherwise, except when a red and white Aramco car whizzed past us on the asphalt road, our bus seemed strangely alone and lost in the vast empty expanses of scorching sand. After nearly two hours, we saw the huge towers of the Ras Tanura refinery looming into view.

There were then about 2,500 Americans in this community built upon a sand spit surrounded by water. Walter and I were to live in one of the bachelor dormitories containing twenty-four rooms, with bath facilities at both ends. We were about 100 feet from one of the finest sandy beaches in the world, stretching for miles along the Persian Gulf. We were within a block of the dining hall, the outdoor theater, the hospital, the commissary and the bachelor women's quarters.

Houses for the American families were similar to apartments or houses in the States. They had one to three bedrooms, usually a combination living and dining room, bath, pantry, and kitchen. They were equipped with modern plumbing, range, and refrigerators. The private houses and dormitories were all air-cooled.

One of my duties was to supervise the American clubhouse, staffed by about ninety Indians, Sudanese, and Italians. In those days of much construction activity in Ras Tanura, there were many rugged, two-fisted drinkers among the American workers. They came in after a day's work, hot and tired, drank a few beers, then some whiskey, and the lid was off.

During the first two months of my stay in Ras Tanura, we had thirty-four fights in the clubhouse, six men removed to the hospital, and a continual commotion of minor fights and scuffles in the dice and card room. We constantly cautioned the Americans against getting drunk in public, and the Indian bartenders and waiters were warned not to serve intoxicated men. But I sympathized with the waiters. I would as soon put my head in the mouth of the proverbial lion as try to talk one of those 250-pound construction workers out of having another drink. Our Ras Tanura security men, the equivalent of the MP's in the Army, were kept busy dragging drunks out of the clubhouse. One was seriously injured when a contestant in a brawl hit him over the head with a beer bottle.

It was obvious that Aramco was flirting with danger through the abuse of liquor. The company had been given special permission by the Saudi Arabian government to import liquor for the use of Americans, and specific conditions were attached to this privilege: 1—liquor would never be made available to any Arab; 2—no American should be seen in public who was under the influence of liquor.

Eventually, Ibn Saud forbade the further importation of liquor into the country. This edict, one of the king's last acts before his death in 1953, still stands in Saudi Arabia.

There were other Americans, however, who had not come to Saudi Arabia to spend their nights in the clubhouse drinking and gambling away their pay. These Americans seemed to find their satisfaction in their work and to take seriously their responsibilities toward their jobs and their country's reputation.

There were people like Charlie Wagener, for example. Charlie had one of the better white-collar jobs in Ras Tanura, a position with considerable authority over a large number of non-American employees. A bachelor from California and a college graduate, he was now dedicated to helping the Saudi Arab to become a part of the oil industry.

"Too many Americans here have little but contempt for the Saudi Arab," Charlie told me. "They run down the country, the government, the people. They're only interested in how much money they can make and how quickly they can get home to spend it."

The room in which Charlie lived reflected the orderliness of his life. He had covered the floor and ceiling with thick Persian rugs in restful color combinations which harmonized well with the cabinets that held his radio, phonograph, and books. He was an interesting conversationalist on a great variety of subjects—politics, religion, sports.

"What is needed here in Saudi Arabia, more than anything else," Charlie said, "is understanding. We must try to understand the needs and the potentialities of the people. We can help them to utilize this oil wealth if we will only take an interest in them as individuals. Actually, the Saudi makes an excellent worker once he's trained."

I found that some of the American women tended to look down their pretty little noses at the Saudi Arab. He was *such a dirty thing,* unkempt, poorly clothed. But there were American women like Blanche Myers who learned the language of the country, cultivated the friendship of the people, and helped many Saudi Arabs to develop their personal ability and resourcefulness and advance to better jobs.

Blanche Myers and her husband, Sam, were among the long-time residents of Saudi Arabia. Sam had been with Standard Oil of California and had come to Arabia in 1938. He had been fire chief in Ras Tanura for many years. His Saudi Arab-manned fire department had amazed Aramco officials by outperforming their American counterparts in timed drills. Sam's tireless training and patient understanding of the Saudi Arab had paid dividends. Sam and Blanche spoke excellent Arabic.

Welcoming me, as she welcomed all newcomers, to her home, Blanche smilingly explained that her hobby was collecting friends, just as some people collect expensive paintings, rare china, tapestries, precious gems or stamps. It cost nothing but a little kindness and consideration, she said; and it took up little room, for it was kept within one-self—and she put her hand over her heart.

To help her Saudi Arabian friends learn English, Blanche conducted classes for them in her living room. The Americans who thought she was wasting her time were soon astonished by her success, for she proved with her students what Sam had proved in training his Saudi Arabian firemen: it was simply a matter of faith in human nature.

"We just have confidence in our Saudis," Sam told me, with a grin. "It's as easy as that. We believe that God gave all of us intelligence. Some have used it more than others. But the Saudi Arab is not different from anyone else. Once he's given a chance to develop his intelligence, he responds eagerly and with remarkable results."

Paul White was an American from Omaha with ten years' experience in Saudi Arabia when I met him. He was a quiet, modest-appearing man of average build with graying hair, gentle features, and a soft, pleasant voice.

"I have always tried to remember that I am a guest in this country," he told me. "I have about fifty Saudis under me in my work. They take orders without question. That gives me a great sense of responsibility. I have found that no matter how uneducated, how dirty, how backward an Arab may seem, he will quickly learn and do what you want him to do with a minimum of training. *But you must treat him as an individual.* This is of the utmost importance. And there is no class consciousness here in Arabia."

One day a colorful old Arab shaikh was discussing labor problems with one of the American instructors in Ras Tanura. They had come to a problem of insubordination on the part of the Saudi Arabs, and the old shaikh inquired, "Do you give these men time to pray?"

"Oh, of course," replied the American, knowing full well

this was one of the requirements of the Saudi Arabian government.

"Do you take time to pray yourself?" asked the shaikh.

Rather startled, the American admitted that he did not.

"Perhaps if you did," the shaikh said, "you would not have this problem."

Frankly skeptical, the American nevertheless took a Bible along to work with him every day for the next week or so.

"And I still do," he told me, later. "Each day when the Arabs take time to pray, I take time to read a verse or two from the Bible. It was amazing how quickly the labor troubles disappeared."

And since then, he added, he and his Saudi Arabs had been getting along just fine.

🐫 . . . *4*

The Bedouin of the Desert

To recapture a sense of the past in other parts of the world, the imaginative tourist might go to see the historically significant ruins or the few carefully preserved relics of the palaces and prisons, coliseums and cathedrals, which might still survive from a former age. In our own country, so many centuries younger in history than the rest of the world, how little remains to show the interested visitor what our land must have been like when the wilderness along the Atlantic Coast was first colonized, and the West was approached by covered wagon. Even the Indians, who have had a chance to preserve their culture intact on their reservations, today bear little resemblance to those proud tribes who comprised America's original population.

In Saudi Arabia, however, a visit to the goatskin tents of any Bedouin encampment is like a visit to the very origins of this ancient desert culture. It has changed but little since the times recorded in the pages of the Old Testament.

Americans, whose mental picture of the typical Bedouin, based largely upon romantic Hollywood movies, is almost a caricature of the "Sheik of Araby"—a turbaned horseman in flowing robes, charging across the burning sands, and brandishing his sword—are right in visualizing a relatively unchanged Arabian culture. But they are wrong in assuming that this means that the Arabs are a "backward" people who have failed to develop any kind of civilization.

The occasional Bedouin who chooses to leave the desert and—for any purpose—apply his native intelligence to the learning of Western ways, is apt to prove an adept, even brilliant student. He often astounds the Western observer by the ease with which he masters both academic subjects and social skills.

The young Arabs we find in our own universities in this country readily distinguish themselves intellectually and adapt themselves socially, blending so effortlessly into this environment that one can hardly imagine them in any other—least of all the desert wastelands they actually call home.

Why are we so prone to designate the Bedouin as "backward," and why do his natural intelligence and poise therefore surprise us? One source of our confusion is probably our difficulty in understanding why these people should cling to their traditional way of life, which seems to us so rigorous and unrewarding. Surely, we reason, they would make things easier for themselves if they could; so it must

be that they just don't know any better, or haven't the
ability to change.

Once we learn that the Bedouin will more often than
not choose to remain with his own tribe even when he has
ample opportunity to choose otherwise; that he scorns the
soft life of the city dweller and prefers to remain independent, we begin to understand that his way of life is not
a matter of ignorance, but of pride.

To be understood at all, the Bedouin must be viewed as
a proud man. He realizes that it is no mean feat to wrest an
existence from the scorching sands of the desert. His ability merely to survive makes him a kind of hero, in much
the same manner that a man becomes a hero by scaling
Mount Everest or discovering the North Pole. The man
who has met the cruel challenge of the desert and tri-
umphed considers himself the equal of any other man in
the world—and probably the superior of many.

Also, the Bedouin takes great pride in the ancestry of his
tribe, which he can trace back for many, many generations
through the centuries. Though he may not know how to
read or write, any more than his forefathers did, his proud
genealogy has been preserved in elaborate detail through
the stories the Bedouins love to tell around the campfire.

My own deep respect for the Bedouin was inspired during my first plane trip over the Saudi Arabian desert—and
was thereafter never shaken, even when I heard Americans
refer to the Arabs contemptuously as "ragheads" or as
"coolies." Looking down from the air at naked stretches
of flat, scorched desert, which I knew covered an area of
more than eight hundred thousand square miles, I found
it hard to believe that human beings could exist there. The
expanses of wind-whipped, sun-baked sand dunes were un-
relieved by any sort of sheltering hills or valleys, except
for a few black volcanic scars in the North and West of

the country, and an occasional oasis of a few palm trees and a precious watering hole. Yet, though I could not see them from this height, I knew that there were whole families and tribes, in groups ranging from one hundred to many hundreds, camped in their black hide tents or trekking across the sands with their camels, sheep, and goats.

At the airport, I asked an Aramco employee why he called the Bedouins "coolies" or made fun of their turbans with the derisive name "ragheads." He shrugged, surprised that I should ask, and confided, "They're the laziest, dirtiest bunch in the world. Wait until you know them."

"I already know something about the way they live," I said. "And frankly I'm impressed. I figure I'd be lucky to last a week out on that desert, myself. I take my hat off to the kind of man that can spend a lifetime there."

The American laughed. "You feel that way because you've just been looking at them from the air. You might feel different when you see a few of them close up. And here's your chance." He gestured toward the customs inspectors, several of whom were tall slender men with long black hair streaming in ringlets over their shoulders— Bedouins.

As I approached one of them, his piercing black eyes smiled at me. He had already started to open my bags. I decided to try out my newly learned Arabic.

"Salaam alaikum" ("Peace be unto you"), I said.

He nodded his head, as if in approval of my accent and etiquette, and replied, *"Wa alaikum as-salaam"* ("And the peace to you").

I thought him handsome in his colorful red and white *ghutra* and long flowing *bisht;* and I appreciated the deft touch of his slender, tapering hands as he went through my luggage.

"Titkallam 'arabi tayyib," he said, smiling. This meant,

"You speak Arabic well." But my obvious consternation as
he went on with a rapid stream of Arabic, not a word of
which I recognized, tipped him off to the fact that we had
already exhausted my limited supply of phrases in his language. He laughed, not at me but with me. Then, un-
daunted by the language barrier, he managed to convey by
his gracious manner of returning my bags to me a feeling
of friendliness and welcome.

Rejoining my Aramco acquaintance, I made no special
comment about it, but I thought to myself that I'd never
feel inclined to call this type of Bedouin a "raghead," any
more than I would have called my good friend Sami Hussein, in New York, a "coolie." Once again I was glad I'd
had a little instruction and mental preparation before my
arrival in Saudi Arabia. I had been fortunate. And I looked
forward to the day when more Americans would have an
opportunity to shed some of their misconceptions about
the Arabs and to gain a little more realistic appreciation of
them before coming to their country, so that possibilities
of honest friendship would be opened up, to be enjoyed by
both sides.

It is true enough that the typical Bedouin is ragged and
unkempt in his appearance, and that the normal routine
of his life in the desert leaves him much free time for loaf-
ing and lengthy, leisurely conversation with his fellow
tribesmen while the women attend to the domestic duties.
But it does not follow that he should therefore simply be
dismissed as dirty and lazy and—by implication—inferior;
this hasty criticism overlooks many of his truly distinctive
characteristics.

The Bedouin is an astonishing example of man's ability
to adapt himself to almost impossible living conditions.
The desert's meager yield of thorned shrubs and scrubby
grass is worthless to man except as fodder for his fire; but

it is converted to milk and meat by the camels, sheep, and goats. These animals also supply the Bedouin with hair and wool from which tents, rugs, and clothing are spun. Since he must first of all attend to the needs of his animals in order to obtain from them the very necessities of his existence, he constantly migrates over the grudging face of the desert in search of grazing land. Thus he remains a nomad, in the centuries-old tradition of his ancestors, for there is no possibility of his settling in a permanent community following the pattern we usually consider "civilization"; his is that land described in the Old Testament (Lev. 26:19-20): I will make your heaven as iron, and your earth as brass: And your strength shall be spent in vain: for your land shall not yield her increase, neither shall the trees of the land yield their fruits."

The Bedouin has little protection against the heat of the summer or the chill of the winter. His clothing includes the *ghutra,* a four-foot square of white or checkered cotton worn as a head cloth; the black *agal,* a ropelike hoop that holds the *ghutra* in place; the *thobe,* a loose-fitting neck-to-ankle garment usually of white cotton. During the colder weather and the months of the *shamals,* or sandstorms, he also wears a brown sleeveless coat called a *bisht* or an *aba.* The younger children wear *dishdashas,* or knee-length white shifts. The women may wear dresses of brilliant colors in the privacy of their tents; but in public they keep such finery shrouded beneath their long black outer garments, just as they keep their faces concealed behind black veils.

The only home the Bedouin knows from birth to death is his tent, which is designed for portability rather than comfort. And yet it is as true for him as for the city dweller that "home is where the heart is," and family ties in these nomad tribes are extremely close and dearly treasured.

The average Bedouin has only one wife, for he could not support others even if he wished to. He protects his wife zealously from contact with the world outside the family circle, according to tribal traditions which evolved in a time when almost any outside contact might represent a threat. Moreover, the ancient code of honor requires that even the men of rival tribes extend the same protection to their enemies' wives and children as to their own.

The chivalry brought back to Europe by the Crusaders was already a time-honored custom among the Bedouins. However fiercely one nomad tribe might attack another, either for vengeance or for plunder, the women and children were absolutely safe from harm, even in the very midst of battle. And though the victors might ride off with all the stolen valuables they could carry, they would unfailingly leave behind them all the food and livestock the women would need for themselves and their children. The late King Ibn Saud succeeded in wiping out the practice of *ghazzu*, or tribal raiding, but the tradition of chivalry remains a striking feature of family life among the Bedouins.

My first visit to a Bedouin camp was almost unexpected. We had been following a camel caravan in our car near Hafar al-Batin. There were twelve camels in the caravan, and we were close enough to listen to the sonorous, rhythmic chanting of the Bedouins as they rode along. The desert heat seared our faces as our car wound precariously through the low, rounded hills of sand. Then, just as suddenly as we had come upon the camel caravan, we were in the center of a Bedouin camp—black tents spaced like checkers on a board, around the dark mound of a water well.

As my driver, a young Saudi Arab by the name of Atiyah bin Ibrahim, stopped the car and motioned me to get out, I caught glimpses here and there of silent Bedouin women in bright orange and red dresses, peering at us from the doorways of the tents. No one spoke. The air was still.

Then an elderly Bedouin, tall and straight with a pointed beard, appeared from inside one of the tents to welcome us. He and Atiyah were engaged in animated conversation for a few minutes. Activity was resumed in the camp. Children darted in and out of the tents, laughing and shouting. Women began to move to and from the water well with copper kettles balanced delicately on their heads.

Most of the men of the tribe, I later learned from Atiyah, were either asleep in the tents or on the desert with their flocks. At night the men would return, and the sheep would be "fenced" in by the protective ring the camels would form around the camp.

I had learned from Atiyah that any inquiry about the women, or request to photograph them, would be regarded as an insult to the tribe. Later I was to find Bedouin tribes where the women were quite willing to have their pictures taken, as long as the menfolk were occupied with other duties, and these women were unusually beautiful, with their veils thrown back from their faces and their solemn outer robes put aside to reveal bright calico dresses.

In one Salubi camp I was to find women with bright-colored jewelry in their nostrils, their hair henna-dyed to a startling copper hue, blue tattooing disfiguring their faces and necks. These women were neither camera-shy nor hesitant to beg for *baksheesh* (alms). The Salubi is the lowest of the Bedouin social order. He is considered neither a Moslem nor an Arab, and is said to be a descendant of those who followed the Christian Crusaders centuries ago. He rides the donkey rather than the stately camel and is subservient to the other Bedouin tribes, mending the pots and pans of the tribes on whose land he lives.

On this first visit, however, I found myself in a camp

where, according to Atiyah, the traditions were strictly observed. My host, Khalida bin Muhammed, was a lean, handsome Arab with strong features and prominent cheek bones framed by gray-streaked tresses and clipped gray beard. Seated facing his intent, forthright gaze, I politely refrained from taking any notice of the curtained-off family section of the tent, where an occasional subdued murmur or sound of quiet movement indicated that the women might be secluded.

Khalida answered my questions alertly and with remarkable candor. Did he know of the fighting between Israel and the Arab states? . . . Yes, he had heard through the tribes of the trouble in Palestine. He shrugged his shoulders. His people should not be fighting the Jews. They were not enemies. He did not believe it would become anything serious.

What did he think of his ruler? Was King Ibn Saud treating his people as he should? . . . His king would always treat the Bedouin with respect. He would share with them what was his. The Bedouin was, after all, the most important member of the kingdom.

How did he get along with the city-dwelling Arab? . . . Khalida laughed. Someone had to live in the cities and villages. He was glad he did not.

Had he heard of communism? Did he know about Russia's ambitions in the Middle East? . . . He smiled. Yes, he had heard about communism over the radio in the villages and cities. He also knew that the communists had no God. If there are two faiths at war in the world, he said, the true faith will always defeat the false one.

There were many Khalida bin Muhammeds among the Bedouin. Wherever I visited the Bedouin, in his camp, on a desert oasis where the lives of nomads and townsmen mingle, I found men of great charm and intelligence. And upon each of these visits, I felt I had stepped back into a life that originated centuries ago—a Semitic life which gave birth to the three great religions, Judaism, Islam, and Christianity.

Socrates once wrote: "He is richest who is content with the least, for contentment is the wealth of nature." Bedouins, despite their lack of material possessions, seem in the very simplicity of their lives to be among the most contented people in the world. Their tribes have produced men of great intellect, although the world has known few of them.

It was from Bedouins of five or ten years' employment with Aramco that I learned many especially interesting details about their former way of life, for they had adopted American ways sufficiently to make a comparison between East and West in my own terms.

Abdullah bin Mohammed had come from the desert to take a pick and shovel job when he was fourteen. Within five years he had advanced to an office job, learned to speak excellent English, and tripled his salary. Now that he was earning over $200 a month, he and his wife and three sons were enjoying the modern conveniences of the new Arab apartment project near Dhahran. When I met him, Abdullah was a veteran of ten years with Aramco; but he vividly recalled the desert of his boyhood. Still a young man, of medium height and sturdy build, he had a sort of ageless dignity now, and his tone softened nostalgically when he spoke of his background. His people loved poetry, he told me, and the past glories of the tribes were handed down in verse, committed to memory, since few Bedouin can write.

What about his own sons? I asked. Did he want modern education for them? By all means, he assured me. But he would teach them himself the ballads of his tribe. He would not like them deprived of a tradition so rich and colorful. They should take pride in their Bedouin ancestry.

Khamis ibn Muhammed ibn Rimthan, Aramco's chief guide until his death in 1959, was older than Abdullah, with hawklike features, a gentle disposition, and an alert, keen mind. He taught me how to mount a camel—after I had tried it the way I had seen Arabs do it, by leaping into the saddle on a standing camel. When I fell flat on my face, Khamis smilingly pointed out that a camel usually kneels to be mounted or loaded. It then goes through many contortions, unfolding its long spindly legs somehow without upsetting the burden on its back.

The camel's value to the Bedouin is priceless, Khamis told me. Some camels can transport as much as a thousand pounds twenty-five miles in one day. Some of the fastest camels can cover a hundred miles in a day. A camel can store surplus food in the form of fatty tissue in the hump, and its three-section stomach provides additional food-storage space. The hoofs of an Arabian camel, Khamis explained, are as soft as foam rubber and superbly adapted to the sandy terrain. They spread out without sinking into the sand. Aramco engineers observed this strange action of the camel's hoofs and were able to imitate the effect in automobile tires, special low-pressure sand tires that are used on all Aramco vehicles.

The courtesy and hospitality I encountered everywhere I went among the Arabs, and the interesting friendships I enjoyed with men like these, were quite a contrast to some of Sami Hussein's experiences in New York. I was embarrassed for my own people whenever I recalled what had happened one evening when I took Sami to dinner at a restaurant on Madison Avenue. Though Sami owned an American suit, for this particular occasion he was wearing his long flowing Arab clothes, including the *ghutra* over his close-cropped dark hair. If I had thought about his choice of clothes at all, I would have concurred, for although this style of dress was still new and strange to me, I thought he looked good in it.

It did not surprise me, of course, that his appearance attracted some attention as we entered the restaurant, but I saw nothing objectionable about it. As soon as we were seated at a table, however, I became aware of some offensive, derisive remarks being made by two young men sitting nearby. The remarks were intended to be heard, obviously. The two were not content merely to ridicule Sami's clothes; they also had a good deal to say about his country and his people. They commented loudly on the Arab practice of polygamy, laughed uproariously over their own vulgar joke about harems, and then made insinuations about the manliness of these Arabs who went around in fancy turbans and long skirts.

I could see that the other diners near us were dismayed and disgusted by this display of rudeness. I rose and walked over to the two youths and said, "Why don't you learn some manners? This man is a guest in our country." But they apparently were not going to stop short of a fight. I turned, intending to find the manager and ask him to intervene. But Sami joined me, composed, dignified. "May I ask that we be friends?" he said, offering his hand to one of the young men. "I do not wish to cause you trouble. I am sorry if my clothes annoy you."

Sami still smiled when the man refused to shake hands. "I'll get the manager," I said, and turned away again. There was a scuffle behind me as one of the young men jumped up to restrain me, then a sharp crack and a heavy thud. I looked back to see Sami gazing down at the antagonist whom he had stopped with a neat blow in the jaw.

"I'm sorry I had to do that," Sami said, helping the man

to his feet. The manager arrived and ordered the two trou-
blemakers to leave. Sami and I returned to our table. I
knew the incident must have given my Saudi Arabian
friend a very bad impression of America and Americans.
Apologetically, I said, "Please don't think that those two
fellows represent the whole United States. Their attitude
is not at all typical."

Sami assured me he would not judge the country as a
whole by the behavior of these two youths. "They seem to
be prejudiced," he suggested, "against my people, or perhaps against foreigners in general. You find prejudiced individuals the world over. I think that mainly they are
afraid of anyone who seems different from themselves.
They don't know any better."

I knew that my country did not have any priority on bad
manners and bigotry. But I knew too that enough of this
kind of prejudice, no matter how thinly spread among the
American population, could mean real trouble for visitors
like Sami, and, on a broader scale, serious trouble in diplomatic relations and international policies.

What was the answer? I thought Sami had come close to
it in defining prejudice as *fear* of "anyone who *seems* different." He had said, "They don't know any better." The
answer, then, would be found in greater understanding.

Much later, after my arrival in Saudi Arabia, I heard this
same general idea expressed by a Bedouin who had left the
desert to achieve distinction as a member of King Ibn
Saud's cabinet. In 1945, he had been appointed a delegate
to the United Nations Conference in San Francisco, where
he had had an experience a little like Sami's, but more
humorous. Coming out of the elevator in the lobby of the
Hotel Fairmont in his colorful attire, the Saudi Arabian
delegate passed a group of glittering society women, one of
whom pointed to him and exclaimed loudly to her friends,

"Isn't he simply gorgeous!" The former desert Bedouin turned and bowed politely to the simpering dowager, and said in perfect English, "Madam, you should see me on horseback. I'm terrific."

The astonished woman would probably have been further amazed to learn that this "gorgeous" Arab had been educated at Oxford, was in the genius range intellectually, and possessed an understanding of world problems which bordered on the phenomenal.

When I met this cabinet member years later in his own country, he told me, "The key to all of the world's problems is understanding. If peoples of each country understand those of other countries, there will be less mistrust and less fear—therefore less likelihood of armed warfare and annihilation for all mankind."

He loved to quote from our Bible. "Solomon put it very well," he said, "when he advised: 'With all thy getting, get understanding.' There is ample proof that men are similar wherever you go, and that understanding of them may be drawn from reading about them. Look at your Old and New Testaments, at the Koran. There is evidence that certain basic moral and spiritual values are common to all men."

The chance to meet the Bedouin, first in his native setting and then in his adjustment to more complex, modern surroundings, helps us to appreciate his historical background and his potentialities for future development. Viewed this way, he seems not so difficult to understand—and, in fact, not so very different from ourselves.

🐫 . . . 5

The Modern Arab

Just as the Bedouin, camped on the desert, presents one with a living picture of the ancient past of his land, the modern Arab, wherever he is encountered—on the job with Aramco, in the major universities or large cities of his own country or abroad—provides one with a living example of the great changes occurring throughout the Moslem world today.

It has been said of these changes that progress in the past ten years has been more rapid than in the previous ten centuries. The major political changes have been apparent—though not always clear—to everyone who keeps up with the news. Less obvious, and just as important to our understanding of the peoples of the Middle East, have been the many social and cultural changes affecting the daily lives of the Arabs.

All these changes, small and large, add up to a strong trend in the direction of modernization. In the entire history of the Middle East, the only previous era of progress comparable to the present was the birth of Islam, with the great reform movement led by Mohammed.

But it is a mistake to assume that today's rapid progress is a trend *away* from Islam. On the contrary, such changes as the emancipation of women and the improvement and expansion of educational facilities represent greater fulfillment of the ideals set forth in the Koran.

Throughout the various countries where Islam is the national religion, the changes in the status of the Moslem women have been uneven, proceeding more rapidly where there is a larger proportion of settled urban population, as in Morocco, and more slowly where a large proportion of the population is nomadic and thus widely scattered, less accessible to the new ideas being introduced in the smaller communities.

King Mohammed V of Morocco, a dedicated leader in the Moslem woman's struggle for greater freedom, explains that there is no conflict between the literal word of the Koran and the many reforms which have been initiated in his country. The Prophet Mohammed was himself a reformer as well as a religious leader and moral philosopher. In both word and deed he was in fact an emancipator of women, and the evidence makes it clear that he would have provided much more freedom for women—in line with his prohibitions of unlimited polygamy, infanticide of girl babies, and so forth—had the prevailing customs of his times proved more flexible. As it was, he left for succeeding generations of his followers a heritage of moral and social ideals which allowed for, and actually encouraged, continual reevaluation of the old customs, with changes in keeping with the times. Thus the king of Morocco claims that the Koran is a living creed, adding that if Mohammed were alive today he would be shocked at the uses to which the words of the Koran are being put by rigid religious reactionaries.

His daughter, the Princess Aisha of Morocco, aware that she and her father and their country have led most of the Moslem world in emancipation for women, nevertheless declares that she advocates evolution, not revolution, and that the modernization of women, "however rapid one might want it to be, must not be a brutal surgical operation, a rupture with the past. The emancipation of women must be done by their consent, not by submission."

One of my acquaintances, Rashid bin Ahmad, a former Bedouin shepherd who in recent years had worked for Aramco and grown accustomed to a greatly modernized way of life for himself and his family, told me that he was very definitely in favor of the many reforms taking place in his country, but he was also in favor of moderation. He reminded me of the old Arab proverb, "Haste comes from the devil," and explained, "The strength of my people is based in part upon the strength and security of the structure of the individual family, which, through the centuries, has been traditionally united by close ties of affection and loyalty. Though we are now ready for great changes in the customs of our women, we do not want to see the family structure broken down by conflicts between the mothers, who cling to the old ways, and the daughters, who are educated to the modern ways."

I asked him, "Do you believe, then, that education should be encouraged only for boys, and discouraged for girls?"

"Not discouraged for girls, no," he replied. "But not rushed, either. In the interests of family security, let the transition be gradual." And he reminded me of another Arab proverb: "Educate a man, and you educate a single individual. Educate a woman, and you educate a family."

"But doesn't the Koran urge education for both men and women?" I asked. If I remembered the text correctly, it read: "Pursuit of knowledge is a duty for every man and woman."

"It does indeed," said Rashid, with whom I had frequently discussed the Koran before. "And the Prophet's own wife, Khadijah herself, was so learned that men came to her from far and near for counsel in theology and law. For hundreds of years after the founding of Islam, Moslem women continued to participate in public and social life, often achieving widespread recognition. Shuhda of Baghdad, for example, was renowned as one of the foremost scholars of the twelfth century. Throughout the Moslem world, women taught school, traded in the market place, sat on the councils of state, and even fought on the battlefields alongside their men."

I couldn't help asking, "How do you reconcile all this with the religious custom of keeping women in the background?"

"You are mistaken," he told me, politely adding, with a smile, "the same way so many others today are mistaken, in calling this a religious custom. As a matter of fact, Islam did not order the seclusion of women. This was a social custom, without religious significance, which was adopted much later on from Byzantium. It is also a mistake—" Rashid smiled again, and corrected himself tactfully, "a very common mistake—to assume that Islam is responsible for the custom of veiling women's faces. The veil, which did not exist in Arabia in the early days of Islam, was an

ancient Babylonian custom, which became fashionable
centuries later in Persia, Turkey, and other predominantly
Moslem countries."

"It was simply a fashion, then?" I suggested. "Like the
styles in my own country which every few years change a
woman's natural shape—but as yet haven't quite got
around to covering up her face?"

Rashid laughed. "Something like that, but the veil was
also a symbol of class distinction, used to differentiate the
free woman from the slave girl who was exposed to public
scrutiny in the market place."

It was interesting, I thought, that the veil, which originally served to identify the free woman, today was the mark
of the Moslem woman who was *not* yet free, in terms of the
current concept of emancipation. And it was interesting,
too, to realize that the current reform movement to eman-
cipate and "modernize" Moslem women was in fact a return to the freedom for women which Islam advocated and
successfully established in much earlier times.

In Egypt today the veil is almost extinct. In Saudi Arabia, by contrast, it is still habitual. It is used to a lesser
degree in Iraq, Jordan, and other Moslem states. In Egypt,
only three percent of all married men have more than one
wife. In Saudi Arabia, perhaps as high as ten percent of the
male population have more than one wife. The modern
Arab, viewing the progress of the movement for greater
freedom for women throughout the Moslem world, is apt
to be pleased with the changes he observes and, at the same
time, like my friend Rashid bin Ahmad, cautious about
proceeding with further changes in his own country with
undue haste.

I had a chance to discuss the situation with my old friend
and teacher, Sami Hussein, when he returned to his own
country after his stay in the United States. I wondered how

different his views would be from those of other Arabs I had interviewed, Arabs, who, though modern-minded, had not actually gone abroad or observed equality between men and women as practiced in America.

Was Sami satisfied with the progress toward emancipation for women in the Arab world? I asked him.

"I will not be completely satisfied, of course," Sami told me, "until both men and women enjoy equally the fullest freedom possible. But I know that these changes cannot be hurried. Our women have for generations been sheltered and protected by their families. They are naturally not prepared to assume too much freedom too suddenly. For freedom is not just extra privileges, such as casting off the veil and going about in public unescorted. Liberty means responsibility. Women who have been accustomed to simple domestic duties and rearing their children will presently be sharing with men the tremendous responsibilities of social and economic expansion in the Arab world."

"Do you want your wife to be an educated woman?" I asked Sami.

"By all means," he assured me. Then, with a flash of his easy smile and a touch of the Americanese he had brought home with him from his job at the Training Center in New York, he added, "Of course, that narrows the field for me."

"How is that?"

"I should prefer to marry an educated woman who is also free to choose her own husband and who thinks as I do about the importance of progress in Saudi Arabia. Naturally, such women are still in the minority here. Only a comparative few young people like myself, men *or* women, are arranging their own marriages, as yet."

Not long after this conversation, Sami sent me a list of recommendations regarding the status of women in the

Arab countries. The list had been adopted by the First Annual Arab Student Convention at the University of Michigan. It read as follows:

We recommend:
1. that compulsory education be put into effect throughout the Arab countries.
2. that curricula be modified to fit the personal and community needs.
3. that education be directed toward clarifying the old customs and traditions, their origin and relative benefits and harms, thereby helping to modify and reconstruct them.
4. that Arab boys and girls alike should be free to choose the type of career and occupation that meets their own interests and needs.
5. that laws embodying, as far as possible, equal rights for both men and women be adopted as soon as possible; that political rights be granted to women.
6. that women be encouraged to master skills which would contribute to the family income; and that they also be taught the essential requisites for a healthy and happy home life.
7. that the use of the veil and other segregating features between the two sexes be discouraged.
8. that community centers for medical care and social advancement be founded in all the Arab countries, and that members of the community be helped to understand the practical benefit of these centers.
9. that educated girls feel it their responsibility to work in rural areas where ignorance, conservatism, poverty and poor health prevail.
10. finally, that all Arab men take an active part in promoting education and freedom for their immediate family: daughters, wives, sisters and relatives.

There are problems other than education and emancipation which interest the modern Arab today. Take Fayez

Jaroudi, for example. He is one of a group of Palestinian Arab refugees who lost their homes, farms, and businesses when the state of Israel was created. I met him shortly after I arrived in Saudi Arabia. He was one of a group of about 10,000 refugees admitted to the country by the king. He worked for Aramco as a bookkeeper.

I talked with Fayez Jaroudi for the first time on the clubhouse patio in Dhahran, under a blazing sun. A spare, wiry young man of 29, with light blue eyes, a quick smile, and curly black hair just turning gray, he seemed at ease despite the heat in his white sport shirt and white slacks.

"I am so grateful to be here," he said, in his deeply resonant voice, his English almost perfect. He had been educated at the American University of Beirut.

"Did you have a family in Palestine?" I asked.

He nodded. "A large family. Four brothers, three sisters. Only one sister and I are left."

"And the others?"

"Killed in the fighting," he said.

There was no trace of bitterness in his voice. His face showed no emotion.

"You must feel bitter about Israel," I said.

"No, I am not bitter," he answered. "I am disappointed that America has allowed Zionism to dictate its policy in the Middle East."

"You believe that America created the state of Israel?" I asked.

"Read the UN reports," he said quietly. "Zionists forced the state of Israel into being at the expense of a half million of my people. It is as if the UN told all your people in North Dakota to get out of the state within a week because they were going to allow one million Jewish refugees to resettle in the state. It makes as much sense as what happened to us. We Palestinians lived on our land for cen-

turies. We built our homes, our businesses. Now everything has been taken away from us. We are the refugees,
the Jews the victors."

This point of view was new to me. "Then you fear Zionism?" I asked.

"With all my heart. It is a greater danger than communism to the Arabs."

This opinion certainly seemed unrealistic to me at the
time, but I had to admit that until now I had heard little
about Zionism as a threat to peaceful international relationships outside the relatively small area of the Israeli
border.

Fayez, however, went on. "Zionism will try to take over
more Arab land so that more Jews can come and live in our
country. The next great war will come because of Zionism
in the Middle East."

"Then this is not something between the Jew and the
Arab? You do not hate the Jew?"

He shook his head. "We have lived with the Jews for
centuries. We respect their religion, Judaism, just as we
respect Christianity. Many of the Jews in Palestine were as
shocked as we at what the Zionists did to us. Our villages
were destroyed, our women and children killed. Someday
America must make a choice between Zionism and the
friendship of the Arab world."

I thought of the many, many Americans who visualized
the Arab world much as I had before coming here: a vast
stretch of sand, floating upon oil, with angry, violent people riding across the dunes, fighting with one another, or
rioting in the streets in the cities, while turbaned shaikhs
furtively conspired beneath the palm trees, hatching endless intrigues. This picture certainly needed revising, I
thought, just as our views on Zionism apparently needed to
be brought up to date.

"How can this problem be solved?" I asked Fayez. "Israel is a fact. It cannot be changed overnight."

He smiled for the first time since our talk began. "America brought Israel into being. It must now bear the responsibility for the victims of the new state. I believe America's challenge is to understand the Arab world. Someone must be the leader in the Middle East. It cannot be the colonialists, Britain or France. We have had enough of them. It cannot be Russia, for we know that danger. It must be America."

"You feel that understanding is the key to America's leadership in the Middle East?"

"Exactly. You must understand our culture, our religion, our problems. You must know the Arab people for thirty years have tried to free themselves from colonialism. You must understand how we felt after fighting for the British and French in World War I, having been promised our freedom, only to have found the promises worthless. You must understand the Arab in Morocco and Algeria, Iraq and Kuwait. You must realize what Israel means to the Arab world."

"And where should we begin with this understanding?"

"Begin with Islam. Christianity and Islam have much in common. We both believe in a Supreme Being. We believe in Allah. You believe in God. Communism and Islam have nothing in common."

Just as strongly as Fayez Jaroudi saw America in the role of a leader in the Middle East, my friend Mahmoud Haramain, an Egyptian, vehemently insisted that the Arab world should be completely neutral, seeking leadership neither from America nor from the Soviet Union.

Mahmoud Haramain was an agricultural specialist brought to Saudi Arabia by the government. He had done a good job in helping the Saudi Arabs to recognize the

possibilities of irrigation, of growing fruits and vegetables
in the desert through cultivation. He was in his mid-thir-
ties, educated at the University of Cairo, and an avowed
Arab nationalist.

"Someday there will be one Arab nation," he told me.
"One nation, from Morocco to Iraq. These people will be
bound together by the things that have always distinguished
nations—one speech, one predominant religion, contigu-
ous land frontiers."

"And when will all this come about?" I asked.

"In one, perhaps, two, generations. Now we are against
things as states. We are against Zionism, against Israel taking any more Arab land. We stood together on the Suez
Canal and Sudan. We stand with the North African Arabs
against French rule or the incorporation of Tunisia, Algeria, and Morocco into a French commonwealth. We want
to stand together as one Arab nation, seeking the same respect and freedom which you as Americans fought and died
for. We want to raise our standard of living, develop our
resources, educate our people. We do not want to be led by
America or Russia. We want to lead ourselves. We want to
be neutral."

"What are the biggest obstacles to one United Arab
nation?"

"There are many. First, the arbitrary drawing of state
lines following the break-up of the Ottoman Empire after
World War I. Second, the lack of a uniform political system. Lebanon, Iraq, Egypt, Syria are republics. Libya and
Jordan are constitutional monarchies, with limited powers
in the hands of the monarch. Saudi Arabia is an absolute
monarchy. There are other Arab shaikhdoms and territories
under both direct and indirect rule. There are long-time
feuds in the Arab world, as between the Sauds and the

Hashemites. The Sudanese are torn between a desire to join Egypt and to maintain independence. There is great difference in standards of education and social structure between most of the Arab states. Saudi Arabia, Libya, Sudan, and parts of Iraq are populated mostly by Bedouins, unsettled and illiterate, who still live as their predecessors did hundreds of years ago. These things divide us."

"And what unites you as a people?"

"Our common desire to be one nation, to gain respect and freedom. We have the examples to give us the initiative. Lebanon has the finest horticulture on earth. Iraq is developing outstanding modern settlements. Egypt has well-organized farms. Saudi Arabia has enviable agricultural projects in the midst of the desert. In the Sudanese Gezira, a million acres bear witness to the most prosperous cooperative farming community in the world."

"In the light of such progress, even though it is still scattered and uneven, you feel the future of the Arab world as one nation is assured?"

"I do," Mahmoud replied, seriously. "And this is why I say we do not need the leadership or advice of America. Nevertheless, while remaining neutral and independent, the Arab nation would wish friendship between our people and yours, based on understanding. . . ."

There it was again: the key word, *understanding*. Yet while many of the modern Arabs I had talked with had suggested, as an approach to understanding, an appreciation of the basic similarity between Islam and Christianity, I was beginning now to see certain other similarities which would contribute to our friendship.

The next time I saw Sami, I talked over some of my ideas with him. "For one thing," I said, "it has occurred to me that just as we consider America a melting pot, so is the Arab world a composite of many types of people. What you might call the original population, the Bedouins, actually make up a minority of the 53 million Arabs in the Middle East."

"That is quite true," he agreed. "It is perhaps not generally known in America that some Arabs are fair and blue eyed, a reminder of the days when the Crusaders were in our part of the world. There have also been Turks and Romans and French and English among us, and they have all left something of themselves. One does not have to travel far to see the evidences."

"I have been impressed by something else, too," I said, "which I think would interest Americans who want to understand the Middle East. That is, in a word, tolerance. There are Christian Arabs and Moslem Arabs living peacefully side by side in some Arab countries. I think this fact would be meaningful to Americans who attach great importance to our freedom of religion."

Sami agreed with the significance of tolerance as a basis for understanding, too. "But it is with the modern-minded youth of the Arab world that your people will find most in common," he still maintained.

I knew he was right. For everywhere I was meeting young Arabs who were developing a taste for Western ways and enthusiasm for Western ideas, who, once the language barrier had been crossed, sounded much like typical young men everywhere. They wanted to explore, to learn, to advance, to succeed. Without rebelling against their entire heritage of tradition, they nevertheless were eager for changes which might enrich their way of life and expand their horizons.

The modern Arab can be found in cities like Beirut—"the Paris of the Middle East"—and on the edge of the desert in good-sized villages like Hofuf, at the al-Hasa oasis. He can be found in the small garden villages, in the larger towns which form the centers of trade and commerce in Saudi Arabia.

At Hofuf I met a modern young Arab businessman from Jiddah, the diplomatic capital of Saudi Arabia. He was well dressed, with a handsome, strong face and hospitable manners. He spoke excellent English.

"How do you like Saudi Arabia by this time?" he asked me, as we sat for tea. Arabs have a facility for good-humored small talk, in keeping with their leisurely tempo of living. They do all things slowly, with deliberation, and dislike any show of impatience.

"I am learning to drink tea," I replied, matching my conversational pace to his. "And to enjoy your custom of sipping it slowly."

He nodded, smiling. "I see you have learned one of our proverbs: 'Haste comes from the devil.' "

I had learned, too, that one should be cautious about expressing admiration for an Arab's possessions, lest he offer the object then and there as a present. So I refrained from commenting upon the splendor of my friend's robe, which was trimmed with gold, usually a sign of royalty or high position. Presently, however, in the course of the usual small talk, he told me that he was a merchant from Riyadh. He owned a fleet of trucks which hauled cement and other materials across the desert.

"Are most of the people here in the oasis friendly to the king?" I ventured to ask.

He smiled. "Of course. They are Bedouins, many of them. They know nothing else. They know only the desert and their religion. I worked for the oil company for six years. I earned enough money to start my own business. There are many like me in the country today." His eyes flashed with sudden intensity. "More businessmen—that is the hope of the country. And more education."

"Does the government want the people to be educated?"

He shook his head. "They are frightened of education. They know it will mean dissatisfaction with the old way of life. It will mean the end of the present form of government."

"But it will come . . . this new way of life?"

"Absolutely. As surely as the night will fall and the sun will rise."

"And will it be a good thing for the country?"

"That depends on a number of things. Will the shaikhs and princes allow it to come? And will the people support the idea of a government under a new leader?"

It is unusual for Arabs to discuss politics with strangers. The merchant from Riyadh, for all his observance of the traditional social amenities and his quoting of ancient proverbs, was, I thought, exceptionally modern in his thinking. And yet, if he seemed an exception to me, he apparently thought of himself as representative of a new type and a new order just beginning to emerge in his country.

It must be primarily this type, I thought, to which Arab statesmen referred when they spoke of the increasing numbers of Arabs who were turning away from tradition and looking elsewhere for new inspiration. It was not so much the old traditions of gracious social customs and tender family relationships which the modern Arab was rejecting as the old sense of material values which impeded progress, opposed education, and discouraged individual responsibility. I could not help but agree with my friend's assertion that the new way of life would come—"as surely as the night will fall and the sun will rise." And I hoped that, in the process of change, the Arab world would continue to respect America as a source of inspiration and new ideas—on the basis of mutual friendship.

♜...6

Lion of the Desert, Ibn Saud

"To understand the Arabs, you have only to consider the character of their king," I had heard people say—usually disparagingly. For, according to the standards by which the people of the West judge character, King Ibn Saud was not a man who would inspire great admiration, it seemed. American and European newspapers were probably expressing the views of the majority of their readers when they denounced Ibn Saud as a lecherous, savage, fanatical Bedouin whose rise to power had been accomplished through ruthlessness and trickery.

For myself, in first setting out to become acquainted

with the peoples of the Middle East, I was unwilling to accept such one-sided criticism until I had at least examined
the possibilities of other aspects to the king's character.

I could agree in principle with the proposition that one
must know the king in order to understand the people. But
I felt that the reverse was also true, and that one should
try to understand the people before evaluating the character of the man they respected as their ruler.

By the time I had spent a year among the Arabs, I felt
able to look at their king from their point of view, to see
him as they saw him and judge him according to their
standards. I was very eager to meet him personally, and in
preparation for such an opportunity—whenever it might
arise—I read several books about him and discussed him
with a number of my Arab friends.

My chance came when I received word in my public
relations office one afternoon that I was to escort two
VIP's, heads of big companies, to Riyadh, for an audience
with the king.

When I told my Arab driver, Atiyah bin Ibrahim, about
my good luck, his young face lit up with a quick smile.

"You are lucky indeed," he said, not so much awed by
my scheduled visit to His Majesty as pleased that I had a
chance to be entertained at the palace. His attitude was
about what I would have expected if he had been con-
gratulating me on my being invited to a friend's birthday
party. "The king is a generous man," he added. "He will
surely give you a nice present!"

I couldn't help smiling at his childlike nonchalance.
"Have you ever seen the king?" I asked, assuming that
Atiyah would not be so casual about him if he had.

"Yes, once," he replied. "From a distance. He is a tremendous man." And he gestured widely with his long
thin arms to show me how big.

"Do you like the king?" I asked.

"He is my king. Of course I like him."

I saved my questions about how I should behave in His Majesty's presence for some of my more mature Arab friends, whose attitude, I thought, would be more serious. But they too spoke of their ruler almost as one would speak of a personal friend—a highly esteemed friend, to be sure, but not one who required any bowing or scraping or more than ordinary courtesy.

"You will enjoy meeting him," they assured me; and then, perhaps belatedly realizing that I might feel a bit uneasy about so solemn an occasion, they added, "He is a gracious host. He will make you comfortable."

So I was more curious than ever about this controversial figure, whom the West seemed to consider a formidable tyrant but whose own subjects regarded him with a friendly respect that was anything but cringing.

For the next few days I pored through the data in the company's government relations files on Abdul Aziz ibn Abdul Rahman Al Faisal Al Saud, the first king of Saudi Arabia, who had unified his country.

I learned that Ibn Saud was a Wahhabi, of the most orthodox and puritanical Moslems. The Wahhabis interpreted the teachings of the Prophet strictly, to forbid drinking, smoking, and gambling. They also disdained to wear gold, silk, or ornaments. They were ferocious fighters.

Ibn Saud was born in 1880 in Riyadh, the chief city of the Najd. His ancestors were fanatic Moslems who tried to enforce in the Moslem world the strictures of the Wahhabi beliefs. They fought many bitter battles for their faith and captured Medina and Mecca.

It was from his ancestors that Ibn Saud inherited his great crusading spirit. In 1902, when he was about twenty-two, he dedicated himself to one objective: liberating his country of Arabia from the hated enemies of his family, the house of Rashid. The Rashidis had driven Ibn Saud's father, Abdul Rahman Ibn Faisal Al Saud, from his home in Riyadh into exile in Kuwait, the little shaikhdom immediately northeast of the present Saudi Arabia. The Rashidis had allowed graft and corruption to flourish in the Najd and were the antithesis of everything Ibn Saud and his forebears stood for.

Having won the loyalty of a small band of Bedouins who vowed to support him in his crusade, Ibn Saud decided in January, 1902, to liberate Riyadh. In a bloody battle the Rashidi Governor Ajlan was killed, and his troops surrendered. Riyadh again became a Saudi town.

For the next twenty-four years, Ibn Saud fought in village after village, town after town, against overwhelming odds, against the Turks, who supported Ibn Rashid, and their modern equipment. He fought in the East, the West, the South, in every part of Arabia, subduing rival tribesmen, consolidating his power. Ibn Rashid was defeated in Hail. The Hashemite King Hussein was driven from the Hijaz. In 1924, Ibn Saud took Mecca, the Holy City, and in 1926 he was proclaimed king. In 1932 the country became Saudi Arabia, named after the house of Saud whose leader had unified it.

One of the king's first acts thereafter was to approve a concession agreement with the Standard Oil Company of California, a 60-year agreement which resulted in the formation of the California Arabian Standard Oil Company, later to become Aramco, the Arabian American Oil Company, in 1944 and to be owned jointly from 1948 on by Texaco, Inc., Standard Oil Company (New Jersey), Standard Oil Company of California, and Socony Mobil Oil Company.

Although I had heard many stories about Ibn Saud's

prowess as a producer of children, I found that many of the published reports were exaggerated rumors. But he has admitted to more than 300 marriages, many of them designed to strengthen the ties of the Saud family with neighboring tribes.

King Ibn Saud, once established in power, was an absolute monarch who governed in accordance with the law of Islam, the Shari'ah, which places the whole administration of the kingdom in his hands but requires him always to conform to "the practices of his Prophet and of the Prophet's Companions and the first generation of the pious," as stipulated in the Koran.

One of the most detailed and flattering descriptions of the king has been given by an Egyptian, Husain Muhammad Badawi, who came to Saudi Arabia as a member of an Egyptian Agricultural Mission:

He is tall of frame and sound of body. His complexion is brown. Dignified of countenance, calm in manner, noble in character, he is a true Arab gentleman. Although he is gracious in society, he speaks little, but when he does speak his words carry weight. He often gives himself over to reflection and seldom grows angry, but when his anger is stirred it makes the earth shake. He is at once patient and bold, majestic and humble, for he detests hauteur and pride. Generous with his welcome, he listens to anyone who speaks to him, no matter what his station, and receives all of his visitors with a smile, making no distinction between those of high and low degree. Those who sit with him are charmed by the sweetness of his speech. A nobleman, he is the noblest of all the princes and kings of Arabia. He never turns aside one who asks anything of him. He looks after the distribution of his bounty himself, rarely relying

on his courtiers to do this. His guests number more than
three hundred daily, yet every one of them is placed at
ease. All over the Kingdom he has set up ovens to supply
bread to the poor, and any man can get two loaves a
day if he shows that he is poor and unable to earn his
living. He carries sacks of coins to be distributed to the
needy during his travels. Wealth in his view is only a
means to attain an end or to win good repute. He is
faithful to his friends and relentless toward his enemies.
He never provokes enmity of his own accord, but if
enmity should develop he will not rest until his enemy
has been worsted. He applies the laws of Islam to himself and to those who are dearest in his sight. He visits
punishment on the members of his own household the
same as on anyone else if they violate the precepts of
their religion. He has a great love for work, but more
than any other thing he loves the worship of God. Never
tiring or flagging, he works without interruption except
for the times of worship and necessary rest, or when sick-
ness overtakes him. In person he reviews all the cases
brought before him by the Bedouin chiefs, and he does
not leave them until the work is done and his commands
have been issued. . . . The only food he likes is rice and
meat, along with certain vegetables and fruits. He sleeps
very little. He rises before dawn, prepares himself for
prayer, reads the Koran, prays, issues urgent commands,
and returns to the reading of the Koran and the traditions of the Prophet. After this he sleeps a while, and
then he wakes up and again considers pressing matters.
Three times a day he sits in his council chamber, once
before noon for official business, once in the early afternoon, and the third time after the evening prayer, when
religious works and the deeds of great men are read. He
also has special meetings with the members of his family

and his relatives. He is fond of them all and visits his relatives daily, conversing with them at great length and showering his generosity upon them. He loves his children very much, especially the young ones. He wears simple clothes of wool and linen. He dislikes silk clothing, ostentation or display. He is an admirer of horses and all sorts of weapons, especially swords and guns. . . . He has made gifts from his collection to the President of the United States, the King of England, and the King of Egypt. He is devoted to hunting and other manly sports.

Badawi's description, I realized, might be as biased in favor of the king as some accounts in Western newspapers had been biased against him. But somewhere between the extremes of praise and condemnation was the truth about the man: scion of a long line of rulers, firm adherent of a religious doctrine which compelled austerity but urged honor in battle, granted absolute authority to its monarch but kept him a servant of Allah, bound by the laws of Islam.

Eldon Rutter, an Englishman who journeyed to Mecca as a pilgrim in 1925 and later spent a year with the king during his initial reign over the Hijaz, wrote:

His personal ambition is boundless, but is tempered by great discretion and caution. He is a relentless enemy while opposition lasts, but in the hour of victory is one of the most humane Arabs in history. As for his system of rule . . . he keeps his own counsel even among his relatives, and essentially his rule is absolute.

Obviously, more than merely superficial understanding of his background was needed in order to understand his deeds—as, for example, in 1953, when the king offered the life of one of his own sons in retribution for the death of a British official.

H.St.J.B. Philby, the Englishman who was converted to Islam and spent many years as a devoted friend of King Ibn Saud, wrote in his book *Arabian Jubilee,* published in 1952:

> Humanity, discretion and caution still remain the outstanding characteristics of Ibn Saud after half a century of absolute rule; and, as for counsel, it was but a few months ago that I heard him quote in public assembly a sentence which is worth remembering as a motto of his long reign: "Take counsel among yourselves, and if you agree, well and good; but, if they do not agree with you, then put your trust in God, and do what seems to you best."

Three days after receiving notice of our planned trip to the royal palace, I boarded the company plane with the two VIPs from the States, and Floyd Ohliger, our vice-president in charge of government relations. Arriving in Riyadh in the full heat of the afternoon, we were met at the airport by several of the king's court, who took us by limousine over an asphalt road to the guest house adjacent to the palace. Our quarters there made the visitors' accommodations in Dhahran seem like something out of an army camp. Here were long, richly carpeted halls with mirrored walls, and doors opening into clean, spacious, air-conditioned rooms.

The temperature that afternoon was 115 degrees, and we waited until nearly dusk to set out on a tour of Riyadh, city of Ibn Saud's birth and scene of his important victory over the Rashidi Governor Ajlan. Our guide led us through narrow, twisting lanes originally designed for camels and donkeys. But now there were American cars everywhere in the market place, mostly Cadillacs, creating an incessant din with their blaring horns. Arab men, women, and children thronged the streets, somehow miraculously avoiding the cars and the inevitable camels and donkeys.

Once they had conquered their reaction to the overpowering stench of the mingled human and animal crowds, our two VIPs expressed an interest in the number-one tourist item in Saudi Arabia—Bedouin coffee pots. We found them in quantity, their bright brass frames polished to make them more attractive. I had already bought my share of pots in Hofuf, Qatif and al-Khobar. The VIPs spent an additional twenty dollars or more purchasing some of the colorful blankets and an assortment of head cloths and *gafiyahs*.

Arab courtesy obliged us to avoid taking undue notice of the women who glided silently through the market place shrouded in black, with veils covering their faces. Occasionally, however, I could see a pair of dark eyes staring at us from beneath a veil. I always marveled at the graceful movement of the women, who walked quickly yet so smoothly that the tassels on the front of their long black abas were only gently stirred.

Our guide's lean, dark face was alive with emotion as he told us the dramatic story of the king's conquest of the Rashidi governor. He pointed to a distant skyline. "There are the towers of the fort captured by His Majesty."

He took us to a gate and showed us a piece of iron imbedded in it. This was supposedly the spearhead thrown by Ibn Saud's cousin, Abdullah ibn Jiluwi, who killed the governor, Ajlan.

Our trip back to the guest house took us through an area where there were more modern shops. New mosques were rising in the distance. An Arab barber was at work, his victim squatting on the floor, unconcerned with what was going on. We passed an Arab tailor shop and a saddle shop, where we could buy the colorful equipment—wooden frames and bags—which one sees on the camels. It was nearly dark when we reached the guest house.

The following afternoon we met King Ibn Saud in the council chamber. He was all I had expected, standing before us, magnificent in his Arab robes. Despite the cane he was now forced to use, he appeared statuesque, even taller than his reported six feet six inches and broad of shoulder and chest. His voice was unforgettably deep and resonant as he shook hands with us and acknowledged each introduction. His eyes were thoughtful behind steel-rimmed spectacles, and his smile reminded me of Badawi's description of it as sincere, wide, and friendly.

As we were ushered into the council chamber, which could easily have held several hundred people, I was first aware of the vast expanse of fine Persian rugs in glowing, gemlike colors. Then, as we were motioned to the gilt and damask chairs lined up against the walls, I noticed that our every move was intently watched by the king's bodyguards in their somber brown-and-black robes. They were armed with gold-encrusted swords and daggers, pistols and rifles.

The beginning of a social visit with the king is necessarily limited to talk about the weather, everyone's health, the state of business in the United States and the world. Sitting farthest away from the king, I was free to study him while he exchanged remarks with Floyd Ohliger and our two guests, through the interpreter who knelt at his feet. The king's face was wide and interesting, his expression often remote as he absently stroked his chin whiskers, waiting for the translator to finish. His manner was gracious and informal, and he put us quite at our ease, as my Arab friends had assured me he would. At the same time, his personal magnetism seemed almost to cast a spell over the entire room. I had an impression of immense, leashed power beneath that bland, bearded countenance, and it seemed to me that for all his candor and kindliness, he must remain something of a mystery, this Lion of the Desert, to outsiders like us from the other side of the world.

I recalled Philby's description of Ibn Saud's youth, in *Arabian Jubilee:*

He conformed readily enough to the normal pattern of Arabian life in those days. There were horses and camels to ride, and hawks and saluqis to hunt withal; there were campfires and coffee to warm one as one whiled away the hours of darkness, listening to veterans' tales of war and love. And there were the mysteries of domestic bliss into which one was initiated at a tender age to keep one out of mischief. In this respect, Ibn Saud had nothing to complain of, though his first bride, Bint al Fiqri, died within six months of their marriage. His memories of her have not been dimmed by the passing years, and often he harks back gratefully to those few happy months.

Perhaps that afternoon Ibn Saud was dreaming of Bint al Fiqri, for when his eyes, behind the glasses, looked far away, their expression was warm, rather nostalgic.

Philby had asked the king about the difficult early years when he had liberated his country from the Rashidis. And Ibn Saud had answered, "Those were after all the best days of my life: the decisive phase, in comparison with which the rest has been easy-going: the years of struggle in the desert, with hunger and thirst ever present in company with danger: not a long period, ten years, perhaps, or a dozen in all; but every day of it full of enjoyment and good companionship, never to be forgotten."

The king's manner became more definite, though no less cordial, when the conversation turned to America and the future of Arab relations with the United States. He spoke gravely and deliberately, and there was no doubting his sincerity. At the conclusion of the interview, which Floyd Ohliger indicated by rising politely when our half hour was up, the interpreter bowed to kiss the king's hand, and we were ushered out of the room. It was like returning to reality, after a charmed interlude in another world.

That night we met the crown prince, the man who was to succeed his father upon his death in 1953. He was big, like his father, tall and broad, with an easy, gracious manner and a natural dignity. But the crown prince did not seem to me to possess the moral stature of his father. There are few Ibn Sauds in history.

The crown prince led us into the palace dining room, the largest room I had ever seen: nearly a hundred feet long, with a ceiling that seemed two stories high. The brilliant light of many chandeliers enhanced the vivid blues, reds, and pinks of the furnishings. Two long tables accommodated the hundred or so guests, with the prince at the head of one table, flanked by our VIPs.

We complimented the crown prince upon the superb cuisine, which involved course after course: soup, meats, rice, vegetables, salad, and finally ice cream with strawberry sauce. He told us that he had an Italian chef.

Presently the crown prince rose to signify the end of the meal, and all his guests promptly rose and followed him into the adjoining hall. There we were served tiny cups of cardamon coffee, and servants offered us the option of having French perfume squirted into our hands, with in-cense-filled braziers provided for drying.

I did not see the crown prince again on this trip, but when he visited Dhahran I wrote a radio script about his visit and recorded it in Arabic for him. He was so pleased with it that he had it played repeatedly on the government radio station.

Before leaving Riyadh the next afternoon, we had an opportunity to meet another member of the royal family, a man who was to play an important part in the history of Saudi Arabia. He was Amir, or Prince, Faisal, the second oldest living son of Ibn Saud and the best known of the king's sons because of his numerous trips abroad. Besides holding the office of viceroy of the Hijaz, he was also minister of foreign affairs and headed his country's delegations to the United Nations and the Arab League.

Prince Faisal impressed me as a man of great intelligence, a scholar and born diplomat. He spoke excellent English and commanded the interested attention of his listeners. He was more popular among some groups than his older brother Saud, who was to inherit the monarchy.

Later, when Faisal took control of Saudi governmental affairs in March, 1958, I was to remember my initial comparison of King Saud and Faisal. Faisal had read the Koran at the age of ten, fought in the desert at fourteen, commanded an army at eighteen, became his country's first foreign minister at twenty-seven. Sinister looking, with his hawklike nose and bristling black beard, he had only one wife and had his sons educated in the United States. Saud was still the Bedouin at heart, although king of his country; uneasy with the power, a man with many wives, a believer in the old as contrasted to the new, a friendly man confronted with problems almost beyond solution.

Ibn Saud, Saud, and Faisal, despite their differences, were men of great charm. Each was to leave his mark on the kingdom of Saudi Arabia.

My Arab friends in Dhahran had been proved right, I

reflected. During our two days in Riyadh my party and I had enjoyed the most gracious hospitality and luxurious comfort. Before our departure, the king even sent gifts, generous tokens of friendship. Driving back to the airport, I was impressed once more by the increasingly vivid contrasts between the old and the new in Arabia: moments after leaving the ornate palace towers behind, we were in the midst of a busy thoroughfare, jammed with automobiles and flanked on both sides by flourishing shops; and then, just outside the city, we saw the familiar symbol of the changeless traditions: two donkeys trudging back and forth in a grove of date palms along a well-worn path, pulling from an old well, by rope and goatskin bag, the most precious of commodities in Saudi Arabia—water.

Atiyah bin Ibrahim was waiting for us at the airport at Dhahran. After we had unloaded the VIPs in the guest house and were driving back to my bachelor quarters, he could control his curiosity no longer.

"And how was the king?" he asked. "The way I told you? A big man?"

"Very big, Atiyah. Just like you told me. Friendly and generous."

"Did he give you a present?"

"Yes. A watch."

Atiyah stopped the car. He turned around. "May I see it?"

It was a wrist watch, Swiss make. I took it off and handed it to Atiyah. He examined it carefully for a minute or two and handed it back to me. He started the car again, and we drove slowly down the street.

"Well, what do you think of it?" I asked, surprised.

All he said, with a shrug, was, "You could have done better."

🐪 ... 7

Training for Arabs and Americans

Shortly after World War II ended, two men, one a Saudi Arab, the other an American from Texas, joined Aramco, the Arabian American Oil Company. The two men were ten thousand miles apart when they made their decisions to take these jobs. Yet they were destined to become good friends, and one was to save the life of the other.

Ali bin Hassan was a Bedouin from the desert. He hailed from the desert oasis, Hofuf. He was young, about twenty-six, slender, with dark brown eyes and a warm smile. He was married and the father of three children. He was hired as a laborer to work on the docks in Ras Tanura, helping to load and unload the ships which docked there.

His first day on the job, Ali was told by his foreman to bring a wheelbarrow from the deck of one of the ships. Ali promptly picked up the wheelbarrow and carried it on his head down the gangplank.

Bill Harper had been with Texaco, in its Houston office, for nearly five years. He was an engineer, had been promoted twice, knew his job, felt as if his future lay right there in Texas. Then one day his boss called him in.

"Have you ever thought about working in Saudi Arabia?" his boss asked.

Bill hadn't. He knew that his company, Texaco, along with Standard of California, Standard of New Jersey, and Socony Mobil, owned Aramco, but the idea of working there—he just hadn't thought of it. Besides, there was his girl, Katy, to consider. They wanted to get married.

When Bill learned the details of the job in Dhahran and the increase in salary he would gain there, he decided that a brighter future awaited him and his bride-to-be in Saudi Arabia. He married Katy, carried her across the threshold of their temporary one-room apartment, and was well on his way to meeting Ali bin Hassan at the Ras Tanura loading docks.

From the day when Ali bin Hassan had carried the wheelbarrow on his head down the gangplank at Ras Tanura, to the day three years later when he saved Bill Harper's life, Aramco's program of education for its Saudi Arabian employees had proved an important point. . . . Ali had been tested for two or three days by Aramco personnel to determine his aptitudes as a laborer. Then he had entered a three-month pre-job training program in which he was to be prepared for his ultimate position as a welder. He studied recognition of tools, hygiene, elementary Arabic reading and writing, and English.

During this period of training, Ali was "tested" on different jobs. He was being graded according to five categories of ability: A, B, C, D, and E. Had he proved to belong in the E classification, the lowest, he would have been discharged. But Ali had fine potentialities. He was a B. He was placed in a "job skill" training program, lasting from three to five years, during which he was trained as a welder.

Ali was a part of Aramco's giant training program for the Saudi Arabs, a program considered unique in the history of American companies operating in foreign lands. This program was based on Aramco's belief that the company had a responsibility to the people in whose land they lived and worked, a responsibility to help educate every Saudi Arab who sought employment with Aramco.

At an estimated cost of $160,000,000 over a 15-year period, Aramco was determined to educate every Saudi Arab on its payroll to the limit of the individual's capacity to learn. This included college education in America where possible. It was education with "no strings attached," the employee being free to leave the company at any time and carry his talents into private enterprise in the Arab towns and villages.

Harry R. Snyder, coordinator of general and industrial education for Aramco, describes the Saudi Arabian program as "good common sense." The company knew that most Saudi Arabian workers were at the bottom of its labor force, few able to rise above their menial jobs for lack of education and training. It also knew that the Saudi Arabian government desired that more of its own people be advanced into higher positions in the oil operations. Therefore, the training program was devised, to insure:

(1) a profitable business operation for the company in coming years;

(2) harmonious relationships with the Saudi Arabian government;

(3) continuation of the oil concession because of the benefits accruing to both the government and its people.

Today, Saudi Arabian workers like Ali bin Hassan study at the American University of Beirut, Lebanon; others study in Europe and in America. Several Saudi Arabs, competing in tests with Europeans and Americans in large universities in various subjects, rated at the head of their classes.

By the end of 1958, Ali bin Hassan was one of more than 12,000 Saudi Arabian employees of Aramco who had worked continuously for the company for an average of eight years. Two hundred and five Saudi Arabs had worked for Aramco steadily for at least twenty years. Thirty-five percent had worked for the company for at least ten years. Saudi Arabian employees comprised approximately seventy percent of Aramco's total. The balance was almost equally divided between Americans and sixteen other nationalities.

Though for some years Americans headed for jobs in Arabia completed their preparation at the Aramco school at Riverhead, Long Island, at the time when Bill Harper made his decision to go to work in Dhahran the company was sending new men like him to their training center in Lebanon. Leaving Texas, then, Bill completed his change-of-employment processing in New York and was on his way to Lebanon for Arabic study almost before he realized that he had left home. A month later, he landed in Dhahran in the midst of a raging *shamal*.

Immediately upon his arrival there, Bill met an American who was on his way home, thoroughly disillusioned after four months in Dhahran.

"I'll give you six months," the discouraged man told Bill

Harper. "This place is hot, stinking, desolate—unbe-
lievable. It's the end of the world!"

Bill swallowed hard, unable to dispute the man's grim
prediction. The suddenness of this major change in his
life made it difficult for him to remember, just now, the
reasons why he had made his decision to come here in the
first place. Fortunately, that same day he met other Americans, friendly, contented people like Sam and Blanche
Myers, whose hospitality made him feel at home and
helped to restore his perspective. Saudi Arabia, he realized,
like any other place on the globe, would be just what the
individual made of it. He could enjoy life here as much as
the Myerses obviously did or be as miserable as the man
who was quitting after four months. It was up to him.

Bill was still there two years later, finding great personal
satisfaction in his job as an engineer and in his participa-
tion in the life of the American community, when his work
took him to Ras Tanura. There he first met Ali bin Hassan
on the loading pier.

Ali, who had long since developed impressive proficiency
as a welder, was doing some dangerous patch work on the
pipes which carried crude oil into the hulls of the huge
tankers docked at the pier. Bill had just completed inspec-
tion of an oil tanker and was walking from the ship down
the long wharf to the shore when fire broke out underneath
the wharf amid the pipes. Ali, still busy patching these
pipes, looked up in time to see the flames surround Bill
Harper, cutting off every possible way of escape. Ali
covered himself with an old shirt, dashed through the
flames, and pulled Bill to safety. The fire was then quickly
extinguished.

Today Bill Harper, his wife Katy, and their two children, their pleasant home in Ras Tanura more than ful-
filling Bill's earlier expectations of a bright future here,

enjoy their friendship with Ali bin Hassan. They feel they owe Bill's life to the man from the desert, but also they genuinely respect and understand him and share congenial interests with him.

The importance of such friendship can be seen clearly in the light of the brief history of the changes that have taken place in Saudi Arabia since the arrival of the first Americans in 1933. As a veteran of early Aramco operations, Sam Myers has been in a position to observe these changes, beginning from the time those three American geologists first put ashore on the Gulf coast near Jubail, bearded and wearing the *ghutra* so as not to appear strange to the local Arabs. Since that historic moment, the fine sandy beaches along the Persian Gulf have undergone successive transformations until, today, one finds communities which resemble some of the world's most popular resorts.

Not only did Sam and his wife have the opportunity of watching the gradual transformation take place; before Sam retired in 1959, they were responsible for an especially attractive change in the scenery. The Myerses were the first Americans in Ras Tanura to raise grass around their house.

Blanche noticed a single blade of grass under the outside faucet along the side of the house one morning. It was probably the only blade of grass for miles around. She nurtured that blade until it spread into a clump, and then a small oasis of grass. She and Sam then began to transplant clumps to other parts of the yard. With ceaseless watering, their lawn eventually became a thing of beauty. Soon the neighbors were waiting in line to get plantings. Today the beautiful green lawns in the American community can be traced to that first blade of grass under Blanche Myers's outside faucet.

During World War II, Aramco's operations were brought to a virtual standstill. Sam Myers was one of the few Americans to stay on in his job. Before the end of the war, an underwater pipe was laid to Bahrain Island, twenty miles off the coast of Saudi Arabia, and a major refinery and loading terminal were begun at Ras Tanura. Peace found the men still at work, in a world now hungry for oil.

The real growth of Aramco—and of Saudi Arabia—commenced soon after the close of World War II. The granting of the oil concession followed close upon the success of King Ibn Saud in extending, pacifying, and stabilizing the formerly disunited parts of Saudi Arabia. The rapid development of Arabia's oil helped to finance economic and social advances.

Sam Myers and others like him were surprised to see the Saudi Arabian government building new schools with trained staffs in many parts of the country. The government established hospitals and promoted public-health programs. It built paved roads, constructed a railroad of 357 miles from the interior capital city of Riyadh to Dammam on the Persian Gulf with diesel-driven freight trains, air-conditioned, self-propelled passenger cars, and modern stations. At the same time, progress in agriculture was speeded by the hiring of experts and the establishment of experimental farms for truck crops, poultry, and cattle. The health program made possible the opening of oases where fertile lands were formerly rendered uninhabitable by malarial mosquitoes. Water resources were continuously enlarged through the drilling of new wells and a widespread conservation program.

Part of my job as head of the Field Public Relations Division was to tell this story of progress in Saudi Arabia. I did it with press releases and photographs, with radio scripts and lectures. The most difficult job was to explain

to the Arab world what this progress meant. Suspicion was
naturally rampant in the Middle East because of the political situation. Many Arabs were reluctant to admit that an
American company could do anything for Arabs anywhere
. . . except take its most precious possession and exploit
it.

I remember a visit to a leading Beirut newspaper editor.
I had photographs and articles on the part Saudi Arabs
were playing in the development of their own oil industry
with Aramco cooperation. The editor was frankly hostile.

"I'll believe your stories and photographs when I talk
to the Arabs personally," he said.

The next week I arranged for two of the Saudis to fly
to Beirut and meet the editor. He was impressed with the
interviews. He ran a favorable series about Aramco and
its Saudi Arabian educational program.

Some Aramco men—top officials who could not at first
be sold on the importance of good public relations—were
as suspicious as the Arabs. Many old-time oil men harbored
a great distrust of publicity and all that it entailed—little
realizing that they were jeopardizing the very concession
they sought to retain by failing to put their best foot forward. At that point, it was not so important that Americans in America be informed about what Aramco was doing for Saudi Arabia. The company's main concern was
with Arabs in the Arab world—seventy million of them
from Morocco to Iraq—who had to be helped to realize
that American enterprise in Saudi Arabia was serving to
raise the people's standard of living and bring a new way of
life to an old country.

It was the far-sightedness of an astute group of executives
that made it possible for a sound, intelligent public relations program to develop and expand in Saudi Arabia, a
program which benefited not only Aramco but the Saudi

government and its people and contributed to better understanding between America and her Arab neighbors.

During 1952 and subsequent years, Aramco geologists confirmed that the separate discoveries of Ain Dar, Uthmaniyah, Shedgum, Hawiyah and Haradh were all part of one immense field stretching 140 miles. They named it all the Ghawar Field. The implications staggered the imagination: an area 140 miles long, dotted with wells each producing 5,000 barrels a day and more—as compared to the 12-barrels-a-day rate of the average well in America. Such an overwhelming abundance of a commodity so precious would be difficult at first for anyone, American or Arab, to comprehend. But to the Arab world, this much was immediately clear: there would now be change where all had remained changeless.

Would such change be for better or for worse? For good or for evil? How could the Arabs understand or evaluate a prospect utterly without precedent? To fathom the significance of the era of change confronting them and to predict its probable consequences for themselves, they would need a complete framework of new ideas.

The communication of such ideas, as well as the dissemination of facts, became the responsibility of Aramco's public relations program. It was important for Arabs to learn that, of the freight that arrives today at the wharves on the Persian Gulf coast of Saudi Arabia, more than half is consigned to Saudi Arabian individuals or companies which have sprung up to serve Aramco or their own communities; that many of these individuals and heads of companies are former Aramco employees who, like Ali bin Hassan, were trained in Aramco educational programs; and that today, they and Saudi Arabs everywhere use the power of their own petroleum in important quantities— more than 3,200,000 barrels of gasoline, liquefied petroleum gas, diesel fuel, kerosene, and asphalt in one year.

These are facts and figures—the sort of meaningful facts which should be communicated to the Arab world. But if the Arabs are to evaluate such facts and interpret this type of information in terms of what it may mean to them personally, as individuals, they also need to be introduced to a whole new idea of progress. They need to be helped to picture a future in which extensive modernization will not necessarily depreciate a past rich in tradition. They need to see that the drilling bit that bored down into the desert sand did more than strike oil: it quickened the life blood of a nation. It produced men like Ali bin Hassan and Ahmed Rashid Muhtasib.

Ahmed Rashid Muhtasib could readily enlighten any of his fellow Saudis who, like the editor I encountered in Beirut, would believe it only when they heard it from the Arabs personally. Ahmed is a long-time Aramco employee whose experiences reflect the changes which the last two decades have brought to his country. He is a pleasant, friendly man with an engaging smile and a warm personality. He began working for Aramco about six months after the negotiation of the oil-concession agreement. The work of the company was only beginning; the first American geologists had landed at Jubail. A company office was established at Jiddah on the Red Sea. Saudis who could speak English were a rarity then, and Ahmed Rashid, who had studied English through a correspondence course, was a diamond in the rough.

Ahmed's initial duties were those of liaison and interpreter between company representatives and Saudi government officials. He settled down to work with the new company in Jiddah. His life continued a normal pattern, or so it seemed at the time. The burden of day-to-day activities obscured the tremendous changes which were taking place

all around him. When Ahmed Rashid received a pin com-
memorating twenty years of Aramco service, it seemed a
suitable time for summing up what had happened to him
since that December day in 1933 when he joined Aramco.

"It has almost been like a dream," he said with a smile,
recalling "the old days." Patterns of life formed from the
accumulating traditions of centuries had been altered. Old
cities had demolished protective walls no longer needed in
the peaceful Kingdom of Ibn Saud. New cities now spread
across land that had been waste since time was measured.
New comforts had become commonplace and the techniques of new sciences had been put into practice, as
though, in the tradition of the land, the Phoenix of Arabia had once again risen from the ashes of self-sacrifice.

Ahmed Rashid is now senior adviser to Aramco's Jiddah
representative to the Saudi Arab government. His children
are grown; one is a student at the American University of
Beirut and his two younger sons are enrolled in the university's preparatory school. Ahmed's new house, enclosed
by a garden compound, is fully electrified from the ceiling lights in the *majlis,* or living room, to the stove and
refrigerator in the kitchen. As he looks around the city,
Ahmed sees the modern concrete buildings which have
replaced so many of the old fretwork-ornamented struc-
tures of Jiddah. New boulevards, wide and sweeping, cut
across the city. Port facilities have been expanded. Abun-
dant water now flows from the Wadi Fatima, an oasis a few
miles away. Government offices have grown in size, and
the responsibilities of government employees have grown
with them.

Outside Jiddah, Ahmed knows that his country has
progressed. Peacefulness is familiar; schools and hospitals
have been established. The distance between Dammam
and the inland capital of Riyadh has been shrunk by the

Saudi Government Railroad. Trucks are carrying far more goods across country than camel caravans. But with the progress come the problems. Ahmed Rashid and his friends are faced with the problem of maintaining a balance between the old and the new. They accept the conveniences of the contemporary world, but they want to preserve their cultural heritage. The younger generation is adopting Western dress, but the majority of men who have passed from youth to middle age in the last twenty years prefer to retain their traditional flowing robes and headdress.

Coffee may be brewed on an electric stove, but the hospitality that prompts Ahmed Rashid to serve it to callers is in a tradition as old as the country itself. His children are learning English, but they continue their study of Arabic, because their father realizes that his sons should build their lives on the foundations of their own culture.

To maintain this balance between old and new is often difficult, but it is being done by Ahmed Rashid and his colleagues. They have, sometimes consciously and sometimes unconsciously, made new techniques supplement and not replace traditions and customs. At the Jiddah airport there is a mosque of trim, modern design. From this most contemporary of buildings, the centuries-old Islamic call to prayer is sounded five times a day . . . just as it is in the mosque near the White House in Washington. This, perhaps, is the appropriate balance that Ahmed Rashid and his brother Saudi Arabs seek and will maintain during the coming years of challenge, development, and further change.

Ahmed Rashid, Ali bin Hassan, and Bill Harper all know that training under American guidance has made it possible for Saudi Arabs to master quickly the mysteries of a mechanized world. During the last twenty years people of this ancient land have acquired many new skills. It takes 850 job classifications to keep the vast desert oil operations going. The services that many of these jobs provide—barbering, plumbing, baking, and so forth—are usually taken for granted in any oil-producing area in the United States, because they are readily available. But in remote areas that is not true. Most Americans grow up surrounded by many types of machines and gadgets, from automobiles and refrigerators to can openers and egg beaters. Sometimes they find it difficult to realize there are lands where such things do not exist, often are unheard of. Thanks to the efficiency of the American-supervised "industrial-training" program in Saudi Arabia, a population of shepherds and small farmers has rapidly developed many technical skills.

The success of this industrial-training program has depended to a great extent upon the excellent teamwork and cooperation between Aramco and the Saudi Arabs. Both have shown exceptional patience and intelligence in solving the various questions which must arise when people of different background and culture work together. This cooperation helped to produce more than a million barrels of oil a day in 1958. Twelve thousand Saudi Arabs and 2,600 Americans were the mainstays of the oil team that accomplished this record.

A further accomplishment of Aramco has been the establishment of an Arab Development Department. This Department has encouraged and developed local industries, communities, and businesses. It has assisted in engineering, technical advice, and planning of private industries and projects. The advantage to Saudi Arabia in the promotion of such self-dependent enterprises is manifest. The potential advantage to the company is also important, as the company would prefer to have more non-oil industry activities taken over by others.

The late King Ibn Saud is quoted as saying, "I am convinced that the West has certain techniques we need. My people must learn agriculture and industry, and if you can teach my subjects to be craftsmen it will be good for the country."

The king's hopes for his people and for the benefits they might realize from American training are already being fulfilled. Today, Americans and Saudi Arabs work as a team in the giant Aramco operation in Saudi Arabia, helping one another and contributing to better understanding between men and nations.

Dhahran, Saudi Arabia, where the Arabian American Oil Company has its headquarters. (*above*) In 1936. (*below*) Today.

Living quarters in the Dhahran area for Saudi Arab employees.

(*opposite, above*) James V. Westling, Ras Tanura fire chief, and Mohammad Hazza, fire-station leadman, check pressure of hydrant serving a portion of the hydroformer at Aramco's Ras Tanura refinery.

(*opposite, center*) The MAAG (Military Army Advisory Group) Mission School at the U. S. Air Force Base at Dhahran is maintained by the U. S. Army by agreement with Saudi Arabia. Here, Sgt. Herbert DeGraw is shown teaching arithmetic.

(*opposite, below*) At the MAAG Mission School, Staff Sgt. Edmond T. Ketchum instructs Saudi Arabs in auto mechanics.

Aramco employes learn English from American teacher. They include Saudi Arabs, Indians, Sudanese, and other nationalities.

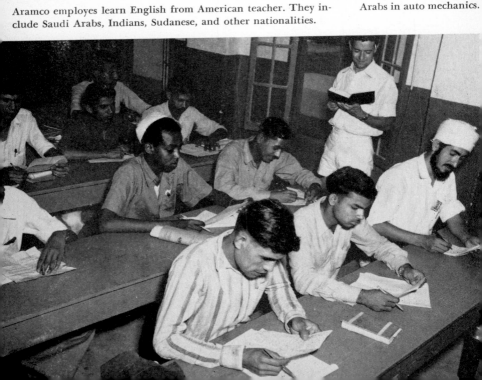

Addition - is finding the sum

13
14
+ 15
___
42

POWER TRAIN & DRA

Seven-mile-long pier at the terminus of Saudi Government Railroad stretches into the deep water of the Persian Gulf at Dammam, Saudi Arabia. Here, sections of a future Aramco pipeline and some lumber are being transported inland.

Arabian American Oil Company

(*below*) A truck used by Aramco exploration parties in the remote "Empty Quarter" of Saudi Arabia.

Arabian American Oil Company

🐪 ... *8*

Vacation in Africa

The paid-vacation privilege which American employees use to such good advantage at the end of their two years' work in Saudi Arabia is considered an important feature of the contract by all concerned.

No matter how much one might love one's work with Aramco, life in Saudi Arabia is demanding. The country is isolated in the Middle East, with blistering heat and barren desert stretching for hundreds of miles as far as the eye could see—nearly a thousand miles from any big city in the Middle East like Beirut or Asmara or Bombay.

Aramco realized that an American signing up for two

years' employment in this strange environment would feel better and work better with the reassurrance of a two or three months' vacation with pay and a chance to go home for a visit in the United States upon fulfillment of his contract.

But the company also knew, even better than the average new employee, that it was important to break up the two-year hitch with a "local vacation" for two weeks, at the end of the first year. Though the mid-contract two-week vacation was not strictly designated as "local," and employees were free to go wherever they wished at this time, the company encouraged them to spend the two weeks with pay at some reasonably accessible local spot, rather than in a rushed trip home, by offering to pay transportation costs to and from any fairly nearby destination.

Despite this attractive opportunity for a de-luxe tour of a fascinating part of the world at the company's expense, some Americans were homesick enough to pay the $1,700 round trip fare just to spend a few days in America after having been nearly 7,000 miles away from her shores for a year.

Most American employees, however, welcomed the company's offer of paid transportation to such exotic cities as Beirut or Asmara or Bombay, or went on to Paris, Rome or London, or Ceylon, Teheran, Baghdad, Damascus, or Cairo.

When my chance came for two weeks' travel at company expense, I had already decided I wanted to see East Africa. I had been fascinated by what I'd heard about it ever since I was a boy.

For months I had been hearing reports from Aramco pilots who flew into Asmara of the sporadic fighting between Shifta bandits who roamed the hills and mountains and the Italian settlers and local British officials in Asmara. Two weeks before I was scheduled to leave on local vacation for Asmara, Aramco warned employees against entering the area: the fighting had spread to other areas in Eritrea, and some Italians and Eritreans had been killed by the Shifta on the outskirts of Asmara.

However, I learned that Aramco planes were still making their regular flights to and from Asmara, and I was apparently free to go ahead with my plans.

I boarded an Aramco DC-3 in Dhahran on a cold, rainy morning in December, 1949, and arrived in Jiddah, our first stop, in clear, bright sunshine and a 95-degree temperature. After a two-hour flight from Jiddah across the Red Sea, we suddenly dipped over a vast plateau stretching as far as the eye could see. Lush green valleys, rolling plains, heavily wooded forests merged into one magnificent panorama, my introduction to Eritrea.

Within a few minutes we had landed in Asmara, 7,500 feet above sea level. The air was crisp and invigorating. The taxi ride to the hotel through winding roads, past native dwellings of unusual architecture, was well worth the fifteen cents. A taxi trip for fifteen cents and all that wonderful greenery—grass and trees and shrubs—a real treat after a year on the desert.

Walking down the ramp from the plane, I had heard what sounded like rifle shots in the distance and had asked the pilot, "What's that? Target practice somewhere?" He had looked at me quizzically before replying, "No. Shifta bandits."

In the taxi I heard shots again, and I remembered the advice I had been given at the office before leaving. "Better go to Beirut, or Bombay. Maybe Rome. . . ." My boss had warned me, "Asmara is no place for a vacation until this Shifta thing is settled."

Well, here I was, anyway, and so far I was finding it a refreshing change of scenery. I was registering at the hotel when I heard the bad news.

"Curfew starts tonight, sir," the clerk announced. "No one allowed on the streets after six o'clock."

As if to punctuate his disconcerting information, another volley of gunfire sounded in the distance.

"They come this close?" I asked.

"Oh, yes," the clerk said with a smile. "Murdered two Italians last night. Right down the street." He pointed proudly.

"You're quite fortunate," he added. "You got here just in time."

"Why is that?" I asked.

"No more foreigners allowed in the country until this Shifta thing is settled."

My suite in the Chow Hotel—living room, bedroom, and bath—cost 40 shillings a day, approximately $5.00 including meals. I felt there was something to be grateful for.

The next morning I met our Aramco representative in Asmara, Major H. V. Stranger-Ford, who had been out of the city when I arrived. He was a likable man, big-boned, heavy build, with iron-gray hair, a friendly smile, heavy-lensed glasses, and a deep, booming voice.

"You did pick a time to come," he said. "But don't worry. Just stick close to the hotel, and nothing will happen to you."

The major explained to me that the Shifta were a group of natives dedicated to the proposition that Eritrea should be returned to Ethiopia. They were attempting to attain their objective by murdering and plundering. The British were doing their best, as administrators of Eritrea, to quell the uprising.

"I've lived in the Middle East for nearly forty years," the major told me, "and I wouldn't want to live anywhere else." He had married his wife Freda in 1917 and for twenty-seven years was active in the submarine-cable branch of the British army. He had been stationed in Egypt, Greece, Malta, Zanzibar, Tripoli, Italy, Kenya, Gibraltar, and now Eritrea.

"I was chief administrator for the British army here during the war," he said proudly. "I naturally jumped at the opportunity to stay on as Aramco's representative."

A gifted linguist, the major spoke fluent Italian and was thoroughly familiar with Tigriniya, the language used extensively in Asmara, and Amharic, the Ethiopian language. He also spoke French, German, Greek, and Arabic.

"My main hobby is flowers," he told me in the hotel lobby. "I've introduced some new plants and flowers here, mainly the gilly flower. You may have noticed it. It resembles a larkspur, with red blossoms. You can see it almost everywhere in Asmara."

I learned that the major's daughter, Rita, who used to live in Massawa, the Red Sea port of Eritrea, about seventy-five miles away, had converted him into a fisherman as well as botanist. "I fish in the Zulu Sea quite often," he added. "Catch a lot of barracuda and tuna."

During the next few days, I became better acquainted with Asmara. I found it a city of proud, handsome, dignified people. The Italian influence was quite marked. There were Italian-style villas and paved streets and office buildings reminiscent of Rome. Women glided along the streets, slender and graceful in their long white robes. Automobiles honked and tooted their way through the crowds that jammed every corner and intersection. In the distance were the majestic green hills and mountains, and only a few miles from the city the lush jungle of East Africa. Saudi Arabia seemed only a memory.

The manager of the hotel told me he expected Eritrea to be federated with Ethiopia eventually. He felt this was the only way to silence the Shifta and bring peace to the country. Eventually, his prediction proved correct. I saw the Assembly Palace where today the Coptic Christians and Moslems conduct the affairs of Eritrea as an individual government. Eritrea is important to Ethiopia because of its access to the Red Sea through its 670-mile coast line and the seaport of Massawa. Ethiopia had naturally felt the hardship after the Italians had taken over Eritrea in 1889, and then the British, after World War II.

I was eating a lonely dinner in the hotel on my fourth night there when an American pilot with the Ethiopian Airlines entered the dining room and, noticing me sitting alone, came over to my table to join me.

"Mind if I sit down?" he asked, after we had introduced ourselves.

"I hoped you would," I said. "What does one do here for entertainment? I'm imprisoned on a vacation."

He laughed. "I know what you mean. Well, you could take the train to Massawa. It goes once a day. Rather dangerous, of course. Shifta have attacked it."

He pointed to a short, pudgy man in a drab, black suit in the far corner of the room. "Or you could get to know Howard over there. He's a missionary of some sort. Been here for several years. He's been trying to teach the natives the 23rd Psalm when they can't even count up to five." The pilot winked, knowingly.

I glanced at the missionary, Howard. Typical, I thought, even to the shaggy gray mustache. The well-worn suit did not add to his dignity. I turned back to the pilot.

"Tomorrow is Christmas," I said. "Maybe we could have dinner together."

He shook his head. "Sorry. I'll be in Cairo."

Later that night I met Max David, an Italian journalist who had come from Rome to cover the Shifta uprising. He was a tall, lean individual with hawklike features and a soft, pleasant voice. The next day Max took me to lunch in an Italian restaurant near the center of Asmara. We were reminded of the Shifta when a funeral passed through the streets. One of the Italians, killed the night before, was being buried. Perhaps a hundred people marched behind the horse-drawn hearse, covered with flowers.

As we left the restaurant I was deluged by a group of Eritreans, small boys with the blackest faces I have ever seen. They were begging for money. I gave them an East African shilling, about fourteen cents. Their faces lighted up and together they chorused, "Long live America!"

That same cry, Max said, could be heard all over the world.

That afternoon we visited the U.S. Army Base in Asmara, known as Radio Marina. It was like a bit of the U.S.A. to see the PX and the GI's again. The base had been in existence since the early part of World War II. It had about fifty officers and several hundred GI's. Most of the GI's were radio technicians. The chief function of the base was to provide weather information for our government radio communications.

I had an old-fashioned milk shake in the PX and a steak sandwich. Max David had a hamburger sandwich and a cup of coffee. Fifteen cents for the milk shake, half a dollar for the steak sandwich. A GI from Arkansas came over to start a conversation. I asked him how he liked Asmara.

"This is real duty," he said. "We like it here. It's a

wonderful climate, and the people are nice. Very few
GI's, too."

I asked him if he had been in Addis Ababa, the capital
of Ethiopia.

"Oh, yes," he said. "But Addis Ababa is not like Asmara.
They don't even have a sewage system there. This is the
big time here."

I asked how the Americans got along with the Italians.

"We have no trouble with them," he said. "There are
only about 17,000 of them left. I really feel sorry for them.
The Shifta are trying to kill as many as they can."

Many of the Italians in Asmara still followed their
normal occupations. They were barmen in the hotels,
shoemakers, dentists, doctors, taxi drivers. It was hard not
to recognize the Italian influence which had given Asmara
a special charm and attraction.

Christmas Day I was awakened early by Max David, who
wanted me to accompany him to a hospital on the outskirts
of the city. One of the Shifta leaders and two of his con-
federates had been killed the night before by an Italian
farmer on the outskirts of Asmara.

As we were riding along in the taxi, Max outlined the
story. The Italian lived alone on a small farm a few miles
outside of Asmara. At about midnight he saw three Shifta
approaching his farm. He hid in the living room until they
came into his house. Then he finished them off one by one
with his rifle. When the police took a look at what he had
killed, they found he had bagged one of the Shifta leaders.

We had to fight our way through hundreds of milling
people to get inside the hospital grounds. Word spread
swiftly when the Shifta were involved, for the Italians and
British wanted the natives to see the results of murder
and plunder.

We were ushered into a small room in the hospital. The

smell was unbearable. Laid out on the floor, side by side, were the three men, naked. The leader was in the middle, a tremendous specimen, perhaps six feet four inches, with black curly hair, powerful arms and long slender legs. Two bullet marks were visible in his chest.

The smaller men, one on each side, had bullet marks in their chests and stomachs. The faces of all three men were contorted in a deathlike mask of hate, as terrible a sight as I have ever seen. But the most disgusting part of the visit was the behavior of the local natives. They queued up in a line several hundred feet long, laughing and joking, and when they entered the room several of them spat on the dead men as they walked past.

I tried to erase the picture of the bandits' corpses by going to church that Christmas night with the British chaplain who lived in the hotel. It was an impressive service, but there were only six people in attendance, five British soldiers and myself.

I had three days left of my local vacation, and the most exciting incident was yet to come.

For several days I had tried to get Max David to take the trip on the train with me to Massawa. For one reason or another he had been unable to take the time. Finally I resolved to go myself, although I had been warned against it.

I boarded the train in the Asmara station early one morning, and there I met Howard, the missionary who had been pointed out to me in the hotel. I had seated myself next to the window at the rear of the train's one car, when he came bouncing up the aisle and settled his pudgy frame beside me.

"I'm Howard," he said, smiling profusely. "I've seen you in the hotel. American, aren't you?"

I acknowledged the introduction and his question. We

shook hands, and I noted that he carried a Bible.

"I'm going to Massawa to teach a class," he explained. "You're welcome to come along."

I thanked him and refused. I glanced at the two British soldiers, one at each end of the car, sitting on raised seats, rifles firmly clenched in their hands. I felt reassured. The train began to move.

For the first few minutes of the trip I thought I was sitting next to an *Encyclopedia Britannica:* Howard informed me that although no official census had ever been taken in Eritrea, the population was thought to be something over a million. He also let me know that the Eritreans were similar to the Ethiopians, but a much milder people. They are not so interbred with Negroes. They are a smaller people than the Ethiopians and do not resemble Negroes. They appear to be more advanced in many respects and not quite so proud. Finally, when I evinced no further interest in the data he was giving me, Howard leaned his head back against the seat and went to sleep.

Halfway to Massawa, the train stopped at a little village station. It appeared to be seething with excitement. When I learned that three Shifta had been killed nearby, within the past hour, I nudged Howard and told him the news.

He did not react, except to comment, mildly, "Someday men will learn that killing each other solves nothing."

The platitude irritated me. "But force is sometimes necessary, don't you agree?" I said, pointedly.

He merely looked at me a moment in silence.

Annoyed, I turned away to gaze out the window. I was thankful for the presence of the soldiers, who were prepared to meet emergencies with rifles, instead of futile moralizations, should the need arise. The beauty of the lush, verdant country outside the train window gave way now to long, isolated stretches of harsh, barren land as the train worked its way down from 7,500 feet to sea level.

I found Massawa a deserted city. There was only loneliness and desolation wherever I went. In the harbor, the masts of ships sunk during the fighting jutted above the water, mute evidence of days gone by.

On the return trip, Howard was waiting for me in the same seat. His face was bright and shining.

"Did you enjoy yourself?" he asked politely.

"Not particularly. It's a defeated, deserted city. It depressed me."

The sun was beginning to set behind the mountains, and the sky was filled with color when the train began the long, slow pull up the final hill that bordered the outskirts of Asmara.

In this rugged country, I was thinking, we would be helpless if the Shifta attacked. I glanced at Howard. He was resting his head in the palm of his right hand, the Bible in his lap.

The train came to a sudden, lurching stop. A few hundred yards ahead, trees were stacked in a neat pile across the track. The engineer began jabbering in Italian. The two soldiers cocked their rifles.

Howard came alive as if he were commanding an army. He gave a reassuring smile to the passengers and then marched forward to join the two soldiers and the engineer peering out of the front of the train.

"Obviously," Howard said briskly, "we'll have to move the trees in order to proceed any further."

"No! No! No!" the Italian engineer gasped, waving his arms. "Shifta! Shifta!"

"It looks like an ambush," one of the soldiers said, ignoring Howard's presence. "The moment we touch those trees the Shifta will come out of the hills like ants."

I looked out the side of the train. Heavy, dense wooded

areas ran up both sides of the hills which angled down toward the track. There was no escape to the rear, and only high insurmountable ground in the distance.

"We could sit here and wait them out," the other soldier said. "When the train doesn't arrive they'll send out troops to look for us. We can pick them off one by one if they try to rush us."

Howard's face was strangely calm as he listened to the discussion. After a moment the soldiers turned and looked at him. It was as if they had known all along that Howard was going to make the final decision.

"The engineer and I will go out," Howard said, "and move the trees. If this is an ambush, they won't be content with the two of us. If it isn't, we are wasting our time sitting here."

The engineer looked startled, as if going with the missionary was the last thing he wanted to do. I didn't blame him. Then, as quickly as he had begun shaking his head, he brightened with a smile.

"Okay, padre, okay," he said. "I go with you."

The logic of Howard's decision did not satisfy me. I could tell from the looks on the faces of the soldiers that they thought he was crazy. I wondered why they allowed him to move, but I supposed they were as surprised as I was at his courage.

Howard jumped down from the front of the train and began trudging up the track, a round, stocky little man in a baggy black suit—hardly the type, I thought, for a hero's role. The small, wiry engineer kept close behind him.

The two soldiers trained their guns on the areas to the right and left of the track, as if they were sighting for some animal which had been heard but not seen. One of them swore softly under his breath.

Howard and the engineer bent over one of the trees.

From both sides of the track there appeared about twenty Shifta, led by one of the tallest men I had ever seen. He appeared well above six feet six inches. He was unarmed. Several of the Shifta behind him carried rifles.

Howard turned, faced the Shifta leader, and extended his hand to the huge, powerfully built Negro who towered over him. Howard's lips were moving. We could not hear what he was saying. For a moment there was silence.

Almost as if by instinct, the Shifta leader brought his hand around in a sweeping motion and struck the missionary in the face. There was a resounding slap which we could hear almost two hundred yards away.

The two soldiers leaned over their rifles and took aim.

"Not yet! Wait a minute!" I shouted.

Howard had been staggered by the blow. He stood now looking at the Shifta leader. After what seemed like an eternity, he extended his hand again to the giant Negro, and again his lips moved in speech we could not hear. The train engineer stood behind the missionary, his hands on his hips as he looked at the circle of natives surrounding their leader.

The massively proportioned Negro stared at Howard's outstretched hand. Then he reached for it. He began to shake it awkwardly at first. Then he began to pump it as if it were the handle of an old-fashioned kitchen water pump. A smile grew and spread on the face of the Shifta leader until he was grinning from ear to ear.

The engineer was shaking hands with another native to the left of Howard. He was nodding his head in obvious pleasure.

Finally, the Shifta leader dropped Howard's hand and made a sign to the natives. They began to lift the trees from the tracks.

Inside the train, the two soldiers looked at me, then at

each other. They were dumbfounded. The passengers were cheering.

The train moved again, and Howard was seated alongside me. The Shifta had disappeared as mysteriously as they had come.

"I was scared, right down to my toes," I said to Howard, respectfully.

"So was I," he answered. He had his Bible in his lap again. He looked at me with eyes that shone. There was still a faint impression on his face where he had been struck.

"It was an amazing experience," he began. "I'll never forget it."

"What did you say to the leader of the Shifta?" I asked.

"When I offered my hand the first time, I spoke in Italian. That was a mistake, even though I said: 'We are friends and wish you no harm.' "

He laughed softly. "Obviously he didn't understand me, but he did recognize the Italian language, which to him is the language of the enemy." Howard rubbed the side of his face with his hand.

"Then I knew I had to say the right thing. I prayed to God for guidance. I have learned only one or two phrases in Amharic. These I thought he might understand." He paused again and looked down at the Bible he held in his hands.

"I spoke these phrases: 'You and I are brothers. My color is different from yours, but I cannot hate you. Will you be my friend?' "

"And that is all you said?" I asked, incredulously.

He looked at me intently. "I said more in my heart. He must have understood."

Two days later, I was back in Dhahran. My two-week "local vacation" was fast becoming a memory.

"How was the vacation?" my boss asked.

"Wonderful," I replied. "Asmara is a beautiful city."

He nodded his head in agreement. "I thought those reports about the Shifta and all that fighting were exaggerated. You were probably just as safe there as you would have been here in Dhahran."

"Yes . . ." I replied, absently, thinking again of Howard, a man I felt sure was still safe from harm, wherever he might be.

🐪 ... *9*

Progress—Problems and Promises

The most difficult job for the Field Public Relations Division during my first year or so in the Dhahran office, and also one of the most important, was that of explaining to the Arabs the meaning of the progress made in Saudi Arabia since Aramco's development of its oil resources. Concentrating, as I was, so much of the time, on the great numbers of Saudi Arabs who remained unaware or unconvinced of the value of this progress, I failed—perhaps it was inevitable—to see clearly the other side of the situation: the special problems of the Arabs who *did* realize the significance of the progress in their country and who were already becoming dissatisfied with the pace of the resulting changes in their own lives.

It was not at any gathering of alert, informed "modern" Arabs that these special problems were brought to my attention, but at one of the most remote outposts in all the vast desert. And it was not a Saudi Arab who awakened me to the urgency of these problems, but a British newspaperman—one of the constant stream of visitors for whom, as part of my job, I acted as escort and guide on a tour of the local points of interest.

The British visitor and I took a DC-3 from Dhahran, headed for Aramco's most distant exploration base isolated deep in the "Empty Quarter"—the fabled Rub al-Khali. Before our departure, my Arab driver, Atiyah bin Ibrahim, had told us stories he'd heard as a youngster over the camp fires of his relatives who had traveled through this strange region.

The Rub al-Khali, we'd learned, was hot beyond belief: stretches of desert without rain for twenty years; areas with water holes four hundred miles apart; along the way, bleaching skeletons of camels and Bedouins who had failed to reach water in time and had succumbed to the murderous heat.

According to Atiyah, the region was also dreaded for its many death traps: pits of quicksand. At night, the towering dunes could be heard singing, he told us—singing a weird lament. Perhaps they mourned for the cities buried beneath them, the famed lost cities which were now and then uncovered by the shifting of the sands, only to be totally engulfed again within a few days.

As our plane approached the mysterious Rub al-Khali, I was too fascinated by the scene below to give full attention to my British friend's seemingly random comments on various questions and issues then current in Saudi Arabia.

But I was taken aback when he asked, pleasantly enough: "How long before the Saudis will rise up against the government and demand more of the oil money?"

I had been aware of some dissatisfaction among the Palestinian refugees who had been brought into the country by the king. They resented the spending of oil money on luxuries by the royal family and felt that more of the money should go to finance a campaign against the state of Israel. But I did not believe there was any groundswell of public opinion against King Ibn Saud.

"Certainly," he continued, "this business of educating the Saudi Arabs, as you Aramco people do, is going to have violent repercussions some day. Soon everyone will want education, and then the government will really be in a bad way."

Despite the reasonableness of his arguments, as he went on to elaborate upon his point, the problem he was suggesting lacked reality for me in that strange setting. And he too fell silent when presently we stood on the end of the runway, watching the plane disappear. It would return in two days to take us back to Dhahran. Till then, during our stay here, hundreds of miles from civilization and the people and problems we had been discussing, we would be surrounded by these endless expanses of flat, empty desert, unbelievably quiet and the air so searingly hot it was painful to breathe.

A few minutes later, we were in one of the air-conditioned trailers which housed the Americans. We drank ice-cold Coca-Cola; then our host, a tall, wiry man in his late thirties, proudly took us on a tour of the camp.

The eyes of the Englishman widened as he surveyed the three aluminum trailers: one an office with electric lights and modern equipment; another bulging with sinks, stoves, and refrigerators—the kitchen; and the third, a combination laboratory with showers for the men. Water came from two outside smaller trailers, which in turn were replenished from a nearby well dug by Aramco men.

Possibly it was the excellence of the dinner we were served that restored our mental contact with the civilization we had left behind. The refinements—and the complexities—of modern living no longer seemed so remote and unreal as during that lonely interlude on the runway after the plane's departure; for the clam chowder, steak, pie, and ice cream set before us rivaled any fare we might hope to enjoy in America or England.

"Do the Arab employees have the same menu?" the newspaperman asked our host—and I sensed that his thoughts were returning to the questions which had engrossed him during our plane trip.

Our host explained that the Arabs provided their own meat and prepared their own meals in their camp. Aramco supplied them with the various foods to which they were accustomed—rice, dates, ghee (sheep's fat)—plus certain American preparations, such as tomato paste, for which they had more recently acquired a taste.

The newspaperman nodded, thoughtfully. "But even though they may prefer their own cooking, don't you suppose they probably envy you chaps your modern kitchen and your other comforts and conveniences? Surely they are by now growing dissatisfied with their old way of life, which might have been all right when they were tending their flocks on the desert, but which must now seem rather dreary in contrast with your American luxury . . . And much more so in contrast with the king's extravagances!"

Our host laughed and shook his head. He had been in Saudi Arabia for about ten years, he said, and he found most Saudi Arabs concerned exclusively with their family life, their children. He didn't believe any of the Saudi

Arabs resented the money spent by the king on the royal family—though he personally would like to see more of it spent on the people, in the form of public projects, schools, hospitals.

After dinner, we were shown the tents where the men lived. Well constructed of plastic, measuring about ten feet square, these individual tents were large enough to contain comfortably a bed, table, chair and floor mat, and, invariably, a radio, for the entire camp was wired for electricity.

The Arab employees had their own tents about five hundred feet away. The local Amir, or Shaikh, who was in charge of this camp came forward at once to greet us in creditable English. A short, heavy-set man with a thick black goatee and mustache, he introduced himself as Abdullah. He gave his full attention to the Englishman's rapid-fire questions: What did he think of King Ibn Saud? Did he resent the American oil men taking all the wealth of the country? What was his opinion of Britain?

Some of these questions, I thought, were rather presumptuous on the part of a man who was a guest in Saudi Arabia.

The Shaikh answered all the questions with impressive dignity as we sat around his fire, drinking the coffee highly flavored with cardamon seed, under a sky filled with stars looming so close we felt we could almost touch them.

King Ibn Saud was a great ruler, the Shaikh said. Whatever he did he knew was for the best interests of the country. As for the Americans taking the oil, he and the other Bedouins believed it would benefit the country in the future. He trusted the Americans, he said, and so did the other Saudi Arabs. As for the British, and he smiled when he said it, he had understood that their policy of colonialism had never been much help to the Arabs.

By the next day, when we set out in a specially equipped Dodge Power Wagon to visit a prospective drilling site forty miles away, my British friend had dropped the subject of dissatisfaction among the Arabs and was able to take more interest in the sights to be seen on our trip. The temperature in this area of the Rub al-Khali hovered around 125 degrees that day. In the distance, we saw a mirage—great blue lakes stretching for miles. Huge sand dunes looming before us proved to be only gentle mounds when we drove over them. A Bedouin with his string of camels turned to watch us as we drove past. On our way back, another mirage glittered and beckoned, this time a city with clearly defined buildings and a minaret reaching the sky.

The Englishman's provocative line of questioning, which at first had seemed out of place to me, took on increasing significance in my mind as our visit here came to an end. By the time we boarded the Aramco plane the following afternoon to return to Dhahran, I felt grateful to him for awakening me to the possibility of difficulties in Saudi Arabia which might well call for closer examination.

When I was able to go into the situation more thoroughly myself, I could trace a very definite change in the negative, as well as the positive, side of the picture in Saudi Arabia since the arrival of the Americans. Before oil was discovered in 1938, the problems of Saudi Arabia were mainly endemic: poverty, disease, illiteracy. Today, these problems are slowly giving way to the more prominent ones correlated with the wealth introduced into the economy by oil:

(1) dissatisfaction among a number of Saudi Arabs with the monarchy, with the spending of huge sums of money;
(2) desire for education among all classes, including women;

(3) desire for more public projects, schools, hospitals, roads, agricultural farms; better use of the oil money;
(4) desire of the Saudi Arabian employees working for Aramco to attain the same standard of living as the Americans.

It was not until the death of King Ibn Saud in 1953 and the succession of his son Saud that any great pressure began to be felt by the government. It came from two sources: (1) the reformists, a group of younger Saudi Arabs, those who had been educated; they saw the advantages of Western ideas, wanted more progress in their own country, more public projects, wanted the traditional type of government to give way to something resembling democracy; and (2) the religionists, the core of old Saudi Arabs, most of whom had never ventured beyond the confines of the country; they didn't want Western ideas, schools or public projects, because they believed that such progress would undermine Islam, destroy the faith of the Moslem and make him as materialistic as the Westerner was believed to be.

In response to the pressures of these opposing factions, King Saud made several interesting moves. First, he recalled all the young Saudi Arabs beneath college age studying in Europe and America. Second, he expelled all employees of Aramco suspected of political activity—Lebanese, Palestinians, Indians, Egyptians. Third, he told Saudi Arabian merchants to stop investing their capital abroad, to keep their trips to a minimum outside the country; and finally, almost paradoxically, he told the Saudi Arabian embassies throughout the world to announce a new program of reform, new schools, hospitals, public projects.

The big question then, as it is now, was whether this policy of reform on one hand and repression on the other would silence the growing number of reformists in the country. I did not believe it would then, and I do not believe it will now. No one has ever been able to stop progress in the world. And the arguments by the religionists against progress in Saudi Arabia do not seem, even by their own standards, to outweigh the urgent need for enlightenment and relief from misery and poverty.

Despite King Saud's lack of training in dealing with the tremendous problems which faced his country and his people, problems created by the introduction of Western ideas, he has the best interests of his people at heart. This may sound strange to those who picture the king surrounded by Cadillacs, women, and an assortment of drunken, riotous-living sons. Actually, the king must, by desert custom, live in ornate palaces and surround himself with the luxuries which to the outsider seem out of proportion to the meager possessions of his subjects.

To judge Saudi Arabia and its government by our Western standards is like comparing a horse and buggy with a jet airplane. Saudi Arabia still lives in a medieval Islamic culture, and King Saud is looked upon as the father of his people. Because of this feeling he does spend tremendous amounts of money on his court, the royal princes, the desert capital at Riyadh, and at Jiddah. The desert Bedouin looks at the magnificent palaces and thinks: "See what our great king has built," while the outsider looks and thinks, "What a waste of money!"

Few people realize that many of the buildings in the king's compound are not palaces in the usual sense but government buildings, state reception chambers, formal dining halls, offices for the king and his ministers, homes for the entire retinue of the royal family, including remote branches of dependents and retainers.

Critics of the Saudi Arabian government frequently compare Saudi Arabia unfavorably to its neighbor, Kuwait, where the utilization of oil revenues for public improvements is quite evident. Actually, Kuwait is a tiny shaikhdom where all the development is concentrated in one city. But in Saudi Arabia, spread out over nearly eight hundred thousand square miles, the same extent of progress could be measured only by assembling, in the manner of a jigsaw puzzle, all the far-flung hospitals, airports, roads, water systems, agricultural projects, power plants, and apartment buildings which have been constructed in the past ten years.

Seldom do those who criticize King Saud and the government acknowledge that, until ten years ago, when oil royalties really began to pour into the treasury, the country lived on the verge of starvation, isolated from the outside world, a scattering of mud-hut towns, fly-infested villages, and migrating tribes, always on the lookout for water and foliage to keep their livestock alive in the cruel desert.

To those who have become familiar with Saudi Arabia, its people and its government, to those who realize how short a time oil royalties have provided the wherewithal for public-development programs, it is amazing that so much progress has been made so rapidly. Construction in the desert, amid plagues, blinding shamals, and searing heat, was expensive and in some cases almost impossible. Everything had to be imported—the engineering skill, the materials.

The change in the thinking of the typical educated Saudi Arab was forcefully impressed upon me when my friend Sami Hussein returned home from the company training school on Long Island early in 1950. He invited me to join him and his friend Hafiz Barudi, from neighboring Qatif, for an evening of coffee and conversation in his one drab, small room in a crowded section of the Saudi Arabian camp in Dhahran.

Dressed in plain dark slacks and a sports shirt, Sami sat down across from me and gestured around his cramped quarters. "Quite different, isn't it," he said, "from our luxurious quarters on Long Island!"

The irony of his comment was softened by the twinkle in his eye and the gentle smile I remembered from before. This was the same mild, gracious Sami, I thought. But it did not take me long to find him more politically conscious of his country, its form of government, its limitations.

What was Sami going to do now that he was back in Dhahran? "I'm going to be in charge of the Arab personnel in the dining hall. I had to come back. The government doesn't want us to stay out of the country for more than two years at a time."

Was he glad to be back? "In some respects, yes. In others, no. I shall miss America. But I am anxious to see how things are developing here."

Hafiz, dressed in a *thobe,* sat beside Sami on a hassock. Hafiz was short and stocky, with a pock-marked face, pleasant manner, and soft, friendly voice. He had worked for Aramco in Dhahran for ten years as a clerk. I asked him what was the biggest problem among the Saudi Arabs.

He hesitated before answering. "Money," he finally said. "Most Saudi Arabs want more money. They want to live like Americans in better quarters, wear better clothes, drive automobiles."

Didn't the Saudi Arabs realize that they had to earn the right to enjoy a better standard of living? They had to work at acquiring education, learning a skill or profession.

"They do not think of this," Hafiz said. "They think only of the oil, which belongs to our country, and the great money you make from it."

Sami agreed. "Our people are beginning to demand more for the oil money, more schools and hospitals. They want to see more progress."

"But shouldn't this come from your own government?"

I asked. "Aramco can't be expected to furnish everything."

Sami and Hafiz both nodded. That was true, they said. The Saudi Arabian government must provide the needed improvements. But the government was so slow. Aramco was faster, more efficient.

Was there much criticism of the money spent by the king on the royal family?

"It is not so much the king as the young, inexperienced princes who are criticized for their extravagance. And resentment about this will increase," Sami said. "Especially among those of us who have been educated in America and Europe—though we know that there is little we can do about our dissatisfaction for the present."

Hafiz said, "I know a man from the Najd who was sent to America. He came back from school with great ideas to help the government. His help was not wanted. He has gone back to America for more schooling—or so he told the government. But he hopes he will never have to return. He is finished with this country."

Sami shook his head. "I may be disappointed in certain things here, but I want to do what I can to help my people."

"I was in Riyadh recently," Hafiz said. "I met a man who is a big merchant. He knew my father. He said the young princes are making many people bitter toward the government. This man wanted to fly on a Saudi Arabian Airlines plane one day to Jiddah. At the airport he found the plane had been taken over by one of the princes. Everyone else was ordered off. It made the man furious."

I had heard, before, of the young princes using their position to gain favors. I knew some of them were abusing the great name of Saud. What did Sami and Hafiz think of this?

"It is not right, of course," Sami said. "It is part of the

old way, and it is hard to destroy the old and replace it with the new. But it will come."

"I have a friend," Hafiz said, "who is a successful businessman. He has sent his son and two daughters to Beirut. He will educate them there and let the girls choose their own husbands."

It seemed to me that this conversation reflected the beginning of the new thinking in the old Saudi Arabia. People were now reaching out for progress in all directions. Only the Bedouin, oblivious of the politics and the progress, was maintaining the same kind of life, although even his life was bound to change as the country changed.

There were other problems confronting Ibn Saud, problems resulting directly from the presence of Americans in the country. I became aware of one of these when an Arab driver showed up at the office one afternoon, weaving and swaying from side to side. He bumped against my desk and faced me with a sickly grin. I could smell the liquor across the room as he approached. I knew that, if he was seen by Saudi Arabian police officials, he would be thrown in jail and probably flogged within an inch of his life. He would surely lose his job.

I took him to the car and drove him to the Saudi Arabian camp. I went in with him to his room and made him undress and get into bed. I found a bottle half full of gin on the table.

"Where did you get it?" I asked.

He shook his head and laughed. "Americans get drunk. I get drunk. *Al-hamdu lillah* (Praise be to God)," he said thickly.

I was seeing tragic proof of what alcohol could do to one of my own Arab associates. A few months later, alcohol brought disaster to one of my workers in the club house. He was a tiny, slender young Saudi Arab with big brown

eyes and a handsome face. He worked for us in the recreation program. He had a smile so genuine we used any pre-
tense to make him show it. He was nineteen and extremely
bright. One night he attended a party given by one of his
friends in the Saudi Arabian camp. He was given his first
drink of liquor. One led to another. His friend who was
driving the car had several more than he did. Both were
killed in an accident that night.

The law of the Koran forbids the Moslem to touch
liquor. King Ibn Saud had originally given his permission
for Aramco to import liquor into the country for *moderate*
use by Americans in their homes and club houses. The
Saudi Arabs could not help but see what was going on and,
as has happened many times before in history, some of
them succumbed to a habit alien to their customs. Teachings of the Koran were forgotten as impressionable young
Saudis became acquainted with scotch on the rocks, mar-
tinis, and old fashioneds.

Although I felt the introduction of alcohol into Saudi
Arabia by the Americans was a mistake, I did not foresee
all the eventualities. A succession of deplorable incidents,
some far removed from the oil camps, resulted in the
king's decree against further importation of liquor into the
country, an edict which still stands, as I have noted.

Problems are not solved overnight in a country like
Saudi Arabia. But when I returned several years later to
collect material for my lectures and articles, I found significant changes. The people were much the same as when
I left them—kind, gentle, hospitable; but the country was
in the throes of a great ferment of change. There was, over
all, an atmosphere of quiet determination, an awareness
of greater things to come.

There had been labor trouble in the country, brief but
serious. Agitators and ring leaders among the native em-

ployees had been dealt with quickly and severely by the king. Some were deported, others imprisoned. There had been unrest because of the Suez crisis. The rapidly increasing popularity of Gamel Abdel Nasser had spread within the borders of Saudi Arabia. There was more talk in the Aramco communities, in the Arab villages and towns, and on the desert about the Arab refugees and the state of Israel.

Many of the people were more independent in their thinking, aware of the rise of Arab nationalism in the Middle East. Many were hopeful of further progress in the country in the near future. Nearly all were agreed that American prestige had never been greater.

It was among the friends I had left behind that I found the change most marked. One whom I had a chance to visit was Khalifa bin Yussef. Khalifa and Sami Hussein had been on Long Island together as the first Saudi Arabian instructors at the Aramco training center there. Khalifa was the quiet one, shy, retiring, a homesick youth of seventeen, earning about $80 a month.

Now I hardly recognized him, trim in his well-fitting Western suit, working as a labor-relations expert for Aramco in Dhahran. He was married, had a son, lived in a new apartment project near Dhahran, and earned nearly $300 a month.

"Naturally I rejoice in my own good fortune," he told me, smiling. "But I cannot say that I am satisfied with the progress made in my country thus far. I shall not be really satisfied until all my countrymen are able to enjoy the improvements I now enjoy."

He looked more like a maturing businessman in his late thirties than a youngster of twenty-four, I thought, as he continued: "I pay $15 a month for electricity—too much. But when there is more competition among the Arabs in private enterprise, prices will come down. Even, perhaps, the fifteen cents we pay for a Coca-Cola!"

Was this kind of modernization developing rapidly enough to suit him? "Sometimes progress must be made slowly to be substantial," he said. "Not many years ago, few of us had ever seen an electric light, a refrigerator, an American, or an automobile."

Had there been much change in Saudi-American relations? "We have always liked Americans. We still do. We are especially proud of your president for standing up to aggression during the invasion of Egypt. We have lost respect for the British and French."

Was this opinion shared generally by his countrymen? "You should have seen the rejoicing here the day we heard the news about America and your president standing for principle," he said, earnestly. "Arabs, Indians, nearly twenty nationalities represented here among Aramco employees felt closer to America than ever before. You proved you were not colonialists."

What of the special problems facing the Saudi Arabian government? Were they being solved?

"The king has a difficult job trying to satisfy both the reformists and the religionists. The religionists don't want progress. The reformists do. More people want money now wasted by the government to be spent on public projects, and there is some indication that this will come about."

Was there any communist infiltration in Saudi Arabia?

"None. A communist would lose his head quickly in this country."

How will the problems of Saudi Arabia be solved?

I was not really surprised when Khalifa's answer turned out to be the same as Sami's had been on another occasion.

"When all of us here recognize that we are all 'members of one another' as your Bible points out," Khalifa said, "and we work together in harmony and understanding, then the problems will disappear and so will the bitterness and hatred so apparent throughout the Middle East today. Understanding will bring the peace and progress we all so fervently desire."

☝ ... *10*

America's Awakening to the Arab World

Leaving Saudi Arabia at the end of my first two-year contract, I seemed to be the only Aramco passenger aboard the company plane, the "Gazelle," who was uncertain as to whether this was to be a one-way flight or a round trip. Most of the others would be coming back to their jobs after vacations at home in the United States. My own plans would not be definite until I had discussed them with my bride-to-be. We were to be married in two weeks.

I could not help feeling, however, that I was leaving many questions unanswered and a great deal of personal interest in Saudi Arabia still unsatisfied.

Later, after our wedding in Beverly Hills, California, I explained this feeling to my wife. She too felt that my experience in the Middle East would have some significant effect on my future career, and could understand why my interest in the Arab world, its problems and its potentialities, remained keen, even after I resigned my position with Aramco and took a new job in public relations in Boston.

A few months later, one of the service clubs in Boston asked me to give a talk on Saudi Arabia. I went through my notes, put together what looked like a thirty-minute talk about the Arab people and their customs and the problems of Aramco, and nervously approached the platform to attempt something entirely new to me: a lecture for the public.

The audience seemed to like it. There was genuine interest in the subject. Within a few weeks I had turned down several other invitations to speak, because my schedule did not give me time. But I had begun the first of several articles on Saudi Arabia for *The Christian Science Monitor*. I was aware of a rising interest in America about the Middle East, and especially about the exotic-sounding Saudi Arabia.

My first article was "New Dawn in Oil Partnerships Breaks Across Arabian Desert." It pointed to the progress being made by Aramco and the Saudi Arabian government in establishing a prosperous and growing oil industry in one of the world's most backward countries. I gave examples of the development of a previously nonexistent middle class among the Arabs. The opening paragraph declared:

The wave of increasingly strong and sometimes violent nationalism making itself felt throughout the Middle East is rapidly forcing the western nations to adopt a new outlook toward that crucial area. There is a growing realization that if the West is to continue to do business in the Middle East, it must take into greater account not only the needs of the individual peoples, but their national attitudes as well.

The article concluded with these words:

Perhaps in the future Aramco will devise a method of presenting the cultural and spiritual side of America for the Arabs to evaluate. This need is evident throughout the entire Middle East. It is a gigantic task, but it can be done.

Several days after the article's publication, I received four letters, which all said basically the same thing. One man wrote:

Your piece on Saudi Arabia does not square with the facts. Saudi Arabia is ruled by a despot who has no concern for his people. The Arabian American Oil Company is there for only one reason—to get as much oil as possible and get out as quickly as possible. We should wash our hands of a country like this. Only the little state of Israel deserves our support. . . .

This type of protest, though dismaying, seemed only to confirm my original contention that Americans needed greater understanding of the Arabs as individuals, and of their national attitudes as well.

Later on, however, after another of my articles had appeared in the *Monitor,* there were telephone calls to my office accusing me of prejudice and probably propaganda motives also. The implication was that anyone who wrote a kind word about the Arabs must be anti-Israel or in the pay of the oil companies.

I tried to make it clear that neither of these allegations was true of me. I had no further connection with the oil industry. I was actually working for a religious movement, writing on the Middle East since I had been asked to by an editor of the *Monitor*.

I further explained that I knew little about Israel but was reading as much as I could to bring myself up to date. I had seen films of the country, had heard many things about the progressive attitude of its people, and had been an ardent and vocal supporter of the Jewish refugees during World War II. Several of my radio interviews for the Air Force during the war and my articles for local papers in Chicago stressed the plight of the Jewish refugees and pleaded their case. One could not have visited Dachau and Buchenwald as I had done without having had a profound sense of sympathy and compassion for the Jewish refugees. But I also knew that there were nearly one million Arab refugees now in the Middle East who were homeless, deprived of their farms and businesses because of the creation of the state of Israel. I knew too that much bitterness and hatred had accrued to the United States because of her part in the founding of Israel. But I had no prejudice against Israel, much less the Zionists, and certainly not the Jews themselves.

This is what I wrote in part in my second article in the *Monitor* about my young friend Sami Hussein:

> What Sami Hussein thinks today about the United States has become increasingly important in the light of the violent nationalism now erupting in the Middle East. . . . Few could put the questions so cogently as did Sami—questions which bear as directly upon our lives in this country as they do upon millions of Arabs in the Middle East. . . . How could man utilize the

vast spiritual forces at his disposal to offset the smother-
ing, almost insurmountable forces of materialism? How
could man advance into a higher mental realm where
an answer to the world's problems lies? How could
Americans show the people of the Middle East that the
United States was capable of producing more than tanks,
planes, and rifles? How could we produce something in
the spiritual realm . . . something important, something lasting? In short, we must prove that we can produce "ideas." Sami knew that the Russians had thrown
the word "peace" around so often that people in the
Middle East had begun to believe it. And they were be-
lieving it in the absence of anything more concrete from
the United States.

The article described Sami's origin as a Bedouin on the
desert and his advancement, in the span of a few short
years, to the position of instructor in the Aramco Foreign
Service Training Center on Long Island, where he learned
to love America and Americans, seeing the best in us and
overlooking the worst. It concluded with these words:

> Sami Hussein knows how important cooperation and
> mutual understanding are to the successful operation of
> Aramco in Saudi Arabia. He knows how vitally neces-
> sary it is for the preservation of our respective ways of
> life. . . . He knows that someday we must present the
> true side of America, the spiritual side, for the Arab to
> evaluate. Sami Hussein is the nucleus of a better world.
> He is the hope of a new Middle East.

I received more vindictive mail and calls following this
article and the publication in *Time* magazine of a letter
of my own to the editors, suggesting some concern for the

Arab refugees. Not all the protests were angry in tone. One, from Virginia, was anxious to set me straight in a helpful way. It read:

> It is hard to believe that in this enlightened age some-one obviously so generous and hospitable as yourself can be so misled. My dear man, no amount of aid or good will reach the Arab populace, for first it must go through their leaders, and there everything stops. Of all the un-told billions that pour into Arab countries through oil royalties, hardly a penny manages to trickle to the peo-ple. Let the Arab help himself as our pioneer forefathers did before us, and then he will receive plenty of help and sympathy from us. The Arab, you must remember, is a backward, aggressive person with little to recom-mend him.

I tried, in my replies to these letters, to clear up some of the misconceptions by offering a few facts and figures on the efforts certain Middle East countries were making to utilize the oil revenues in improving the lot of their peo-ples. And I was heartened by an occasional letter express-ing genuine interest in the subject. One letter, from Iquitos, Peru, thanked me for calling attention, in the *Time* col-umn, to the plight of the "thousands of homeless, starving Arabs" and agreed that people throughout the world needed a clearer understanding of this situation.

In the summer of 1952 I returned to California and joined a West Coast oil corporation. My public relations duties included a considerable number of talks each year before service clubs and other organizations on the subject of oil production in the state of California. During this period I was invited by several executives of my corpora-tion to speak to some of these groups about Saudi Arabia.

I kept these talks extremely general, dealing with the customs of the country and the problems of the Saudi Arab, avoiding any mention of the state of Israel or the rise of Arab nationalism. However, I was becoming aware that American opinion was awakening almost overnight to the importance of the Middle East and its vast oil resources.

I remembered a poll taken in 1948 while the Palestine war between the Arabs and the Israelis raged. Forty-two percent of those polled had no opinion as to who was in the right. Thirteen percent said both sides were in the wrong. The same year, seventy-three percent of those polled said the United States should not send arms to either Israel or the Arabs. Twelve percent said they didn't know which side should get American aid. In 1952, only half of a cross section of Americans who were asked, "How important is the Middle East to the United States?" said that it was important. In another poll the same year, ninety percent of a group of Americans could not identify Islam, the religion of the Arab world, nor could they identify Mohammed, the founder of Islam, or some of its basic precepts. In still another poll in 1953, a group of Americans were asked to name the countries of the Middle East. Fewer than half could name more than one country.

Questions asked by members of my audiences in those days about Saudi Arabia and the Middle East reflected this general lack of knowledge. Even more appalling to me was the lack of interest and information about the Middle East on the part of some of the top executives in oil companies with tremendous holdings in the Arab world. And there was a disappointing lack of initiative on the part of the industry, reflected in my own case by the number of talks I gave for other large companies, who had no apparent inclination to develop a program of sound, sensible public relations pertaining to the Arab world.

With the increasing requests for my talk on Saudi Arabia and an expanded speaking schedule for my own corporation, I decided to obtain an agent, cut down on the free talks, and take a limited number of engagements with larger groups, college forums, women's clubs, management organizations. A portion of my fees was donated to the Arab refugee fund, to the support of several refugee children in Jordan, and to the American Friends of the Middle East in New York.

I had become interested in the AFME through my former "boss," Major General Russell L. Maxwell, then senior vice-president of the American Machine and Foundry Company, and former assistant chief of staff, G-4, of the Army under Generals Marshall and Eisenhower. As a young second lieutenant in the early days of World War II, I had met General Maxwell at Camp Ellis, Illinois, upon his return from Cairo, where he had been the first American general in the Middle East. Having been put in charge of the radio programs at the camp, I came into close contact with the general and had some opportunity to learn his personal views and sentiments. I was therefore naturally impressed when General Maxwell became one of the sponsors of the American Friends of the Middle East, an organization of independent Americans who believe:

> Peace can be waged, at least in part, by a better understanding of the religious, cultural and social aspirations of people in other parts of the world. Our interest lies in the peoples of the Middle East. We believe that our great civilizations in the Middle East and West derive their strength essentially from the same wellsprings and that a better mutual understanding between Americans and the people living between Morocco and Indonesia will result in greater harmony of action.

Essentially, I found the AFME an organization dedicated to telling the American people the truth about the Arab world and the Middle East. I felt proud to be a member of an organization which included such people as Lowell Thomas; Dorothy Thompson; Dr. Edward L. R. Elson, President Eisenhower's pastor in Washington, D.C.; Harold Lamb, and a host of distinguished educators, executives and just plain Americans interested in the Arab world and the truth.

The nature of the work in which I was already engaged made me acutely aware of the need for such an organization, especially since I was now, more frequently than ever before, encountering examples of the kind of misinformation being given the American people.

A typical distortion was presented to a large audience in Los Angeles in 1956 by a well-known lecturer who had never been to Saudi Arabia and had never met the king; "King Saud is a gutter ape, a weak despot who leans toward communism and sits on his fading throne passing out millions of dollars to his illiterate sons, adding to his harem daily, a man completely devoid of responsibility to his people."

As a member of the United States Air Force Reserve I sat one night in my squadron meeting in West Los Angeles to hear a former United States Congressman say: "I know Saud. I met him in Arabia. He is a wicked man. He has no sense of values. I watched him at the Dhahran airport passing out money to thousands of beggars. Saudi Arabia is a terrible place filled with misery and ignorance. Its king despises America. Its people love communism." This self-styled authority on Saudi Arabia had visited the country for several hours on a trip to the Middle East. He had never talked with King Saud. Obviously he was appealing for votes.

Inevitably, a certain percentage of the listeners would believe speakers like these. Fortunately, other Americans were objective. Joseph Alsop, for example, reported after a visit with King Saud:

> The king's words of friendship for America are obviously sincere. . . . One gets a sense of the king's character and of his predicament, a sense of a good man born in old ways, attached to all that is customary and familiar, yet required by fate to carry his country through the baffling transition from the past into the present.

Wanda Jablonski, an editor of *Petroleum Week*, wrote:

> He is a good man, with a simple, straightforward manner, who tries hard to be a good father to his people. . . . He is powerful—but he is no dictator. His position has been aptly described as "autocratic in theory but democratic in principle. . . ." He is deeply religious—with no sham about it. . . . He has emerged as an Arab ruler who keeps his feet on the ground, a staunch opponent of communism, a friend of America.

Just at the time when my lectures on Saudi Arabia were increasing in number, a flood of propaganda against the Saudi government seemed to inundate the country, reaching a climax early in 1957 when King Saud visited America as a guest of President Eisenhower. Many discourteous remarks were directed toward the king by Zionists, Mayor Wagner of New York City, and other politicians whose ears were tuned to the groundswell of opposition, hoping they might pick up some votes in the next election.

All kinds of charges were hurled at the king. He was a slave trader, anti-Jewish, anti-Catholic, anti-Christian—in short, a monster. New York City officially refused to receive him. No one in the city government seemed to realize they were embarrassing the United States government, the president of the United States, and the head of a foreign state where America maintained an air base near the borders of the Soviet Union and where American industry had helped to develop one of the world's most valued oil concessions, oil of vital importance to the security of America and the free world.

Fortunately, a gracious and hospitable man in the White House managed to counter the effects of this un-American reception. King Saud's visit was a success, and his crippled young son, Prince Mashur, was taken to the hearts of the American people.

What about the charges leveled at King Saud and his government? Was he anti-Catholic, anti-Christian? Was there no freedom of worship in Saudi Arabia? As a Protestant, I went to church almost every week in Saudi Arabia. My Catholic friends went to mass. No one ever stopped me from worship, and I knew of no one else stopped from worship. It is true that American missionaries were not allowed in the country. But Saudi Arabia, home of Islam, home of Mecca, the holy city, felt that its religion was adequate for its people, and did not want Moslems converted into Christians.

King Saud does not permit American Jews within his borders. His reason is this:

Since we are technically still at war with the state of Israel, and since Israel is financed, governed, and dominated by Zionists, who have caused the displacement of nearly one million Arabs from Palestine, we cannot take the chance of having American Zionists, who support Israel, in our country as a subversive force.

It is true that slavery exists in Saudi Arabia. King Saud is sincere in his desire to rid the country of slavery, but it has existed for years, is recognized by the Koran and Islam, and therefore cannot be eradicated overnight. He has taken firm steps to have slavery outlawed. He is not a "slave trader."

To read some of the magazine articles about slavery in Saudi Arabia, one would assume that the country is overrun with slaves. The much respected *Saturday Evening Post* did not contribute to better understanding of the slavery problem in Saudi Arabia with the publication of an article by Noel Barber in its November 30, 1957, edition, entitled "I Learned Slavery Isn't Dead."

The best answer to Mr. Barber's misleading article came from Dr. George Rentz, the adviser on Arab affairs to Aramco, who has lived in Saudi Arabia for nearly fifteen years. He wrote:

Noel Barber's figure of "at least 500,000" slaves in Saudi Arabia would mean that one out of every ten or a dozen persons in the country is a slave. If this were so, it would be difficult to go about in any town or crowd without bumping into slaves right and left. Anyone who has spent appreciable time in Saudi Arabia knows how ridiculous this is.

Dr. Rentz then goes on to point out in his documented report:

For more than twenty years the importation of slaves into Saudi Arabia has been forbidden by law. Violations of this law are few and far between, and its maintenance means that the institution of slavery is bound to wither away. . . ."

Dr. Rentz sketched the background of slavery in his report, its recognition by Islam, its role in the Bible and in the history of the Jewish people. Slaves in Arabia are family retainers treated as members of the household. Rather than being given menial tasks, they are, because of their customary devotion to their masters, placed in positions of trust. Many slaves have declined to accept freedom when it has been offered to them. One of the highest members of the Saudi Arabian government in recent years was a man descended from slaves.

To demonstrate Noel Barber's unreliability, Dr. Rentz quoted contradictions and inconsistencies from Barber's articles printed in the *London Daily Mail*. Continuing in his report to point out the inaccuracies in Barber's article, Dr. Rentz stated:

> Americans who have lived in Saudi Arabia for years will find it hard to believe Barber's stories of flourishing slave markets in Saudi Arabia. Not only have they not seen such markets, but they have no convincing hearsay evidence of their existence. . . .

President Eisenhower has said, "You do not have to agree with a man to be his friend." Surely, though we may disagree with some people and some institutions of the Arab world today, and of Israel, we do not have to be their enemies.

King Saud, Prince Faisal, and other Arab leaders have become increasingly aware of the deficiencies of their respective governments. But they deserve praise for what they have accomplished thus far, and encouragement for the difficulties ahead.

As citizens of a nation whose Constitution guarantees us freedom of speech, we all have the right to express our personal views, pro or con, on any question. But this cherished freedom is also a grave responsibility. It behooves us to check on the validity of our views, and when in doubt to seek further information before letting ourselves be influenced by deliberate, possibly ulteriorly motivated, distortions. When the subject in question is one of such manifest importance as the Middle East, we should be especially thorough in examining the issues: not only because we value the truth and abhor deception; not only because we dare not condemn as enemies those who need and deserve our friendship; but also for reasons of enlightened self-interest—because these issues directly and vitally involve our own national welfare.

𓃝 ... *11*

Arab Nationalism, Zionism, and Communism

For me, and probably for the majority of Americans who have spent time in Aramco communities in Saudi Arabia during the past ten years, it is difficult now to realize that we were actually living, during this time, in the near vicinity of an event of such historic significance as the conflict in Palestine. The sound and fury attending the birth of the new state of Israel were perhaps muffled, for us, by the vast expanses of empty desert surrounding us. And the Saudi Arabs who were our immediate neighbors were themselves not well aware of the implications of the struggle. Serious though the results were to prove, for the Arab world and ultimately for the rest of the world, the Saudi Arabs, limited by lack of education and lack of modern communication, seemed for the most part to know little and care less about the meaning of Israel. We Americans living among them during that period also remained comparatively uninformed and unconcerned—strange as it now seems in retrospect.

It was not until after I had returned to the United States from Saudi Arabia for the first time that I became fully alert to the reality of this conflict—for it became my duty, in connection with my lectures, to acquaint myself with the facts about Israel.

The Palestine problem did not first arise in 1947, as so many people believe. It actually began in 1917, when the British, who were engaged in liberating Palestine from the Ottoman Empire, promised the Jews a national home, then failed to follow through. The British were unable to restore order in the resulting discord between Jews and Arabs. Thereafter, until 1947, the British were in the position of indecisive and ineffectual middlemen, helpless to resolve the impasse between the Palestine Arabs who had been the dominant majority in the area for centuries, and the Zionists who were firm in their demand for a Jewish national home in the midst of Arab territory.

That the Zionists were ultimately able to exert the decisive pressure in this deadlock is lucidly explained in Erich W. Bethmann's *Decisive Years in Palestine, 1918-1948,* number thirteen of the Minaret series published by American Friends of the Middle East. As director of Research and Publications, Dr. Bethmann draws an accurate and vivid picture of the events which took place over a thirty-year period in the Holy Land. He writes in part:

On April 28, 1947, the Special Session of the General Assembly of the United Nations convened at Lake Suc-

cess to consider Palestine. A committee was appointed to
investigate the situation and report to the second regular
session of the General Assembly in September 1947.
During this period and during the following United Nations sessions, Zionist pressures were increasingly exercised. The American Jewish Conference, the American
Jewish Committee, the American Christian Palestine
Committee, the Jewish National Council, the American
section of the Jewish agency for Palestine, all urged UN
action favorable to the Jews. The C.I.O. pledged its support. The American public was led to believe that the
Palestine underground was engaged in the same kind of
struggle as the American Revolutionists had waged
against the very same imperialistic power and that the
establishment of an independent Jewish commonwealth
in Palestine would be one of the loftiest acts of human-
itarianism.

. . . the few dissenting voices were hardly audible.
One was . . . that of Dr. Judah L. Magnes, the President of the Hebrew University in Jerusalem. He pleaded
for a bi-national state that would not divide Palestine
but would reconcile both nationalist factions. The re-
generated Jerusalem for which he prayed was to be
gained only through understanding and cooperation between Jew and Arab, never by force and violence. Another was that of the American Council for Judaism,
which submitted a memorandum to the Secretary of
State, George C. Marshall, opposing the establishment
of a Jewish state in Palestine—or anywhere else—
pointing to the grave dangers such a course of action
would engender. They rejected especially the claim of
the Jewish Agency as "a body representing the Jewish
people" to participate in the United Nations delibera-
tions. The Arabs had almost no voice at all in the United

States. There was an Institute of Arab-American affairs which published a dignified quarterly called *The Arab World*. This blended ancient Arab achievements with new national aspirations, but it had no influence on American opinion. The only other American group was the Committee for Justice and Peace in the Holy Land, under the leadership of Dean Virginia Gildersleeve of Barnard College. It pleaded that the voice of the Palestinian Arabs—a two-thirds majority of the inhabitants of that country at the time—should be heard, their rights respected and their security guaranteed; otherwise the United Nations at its very outset would become a partner in committing a grave injustice, which might have unfortunate consequences not only for Palestine, but also for the harmonious functioning of the newly born world organization. . . .

The United Nations Special Committee on Palestine (UNSCOP) after conducting its inquiry was not able to present a unanimous report. [Finally, a partition scheme was presented. The partition plan assigned fifty-six percent of the area to the Jewish state. About 497,000 Arabs would be left in this area.]

The final vote [on the partition proposal] was scheduled for November 26, following a night session at which the debate was to be concluded. But the night session was canceled after the Zionists ascertained that they lacked possible assurance of the necessary two-thirds. The next day was Thanksgiving Day. The delay provided forty-eight additional hours for lobbying. During these forty-eight hours Zionist statesmen, members of parliaments, and influential Zionists in all countries were called by long distance telephone to bring pressure to bear on their delegations. . . . On the morning of November 29, the partition was accepted by a vote of thirty-three to thirteen, with ten abstentions and one absent . . . Liberia had shifted her vote, also Haiti and the Philippines, who only twenty-four hours before had fiercely attacked the majority proposal. The pressures exerted on these states and others are described . . . in Alfred M. Lilienthal's book, *What Price Israel?* . . . The United States and Soviet Russia both voted for partition.

Doubtless the objectives of those who sponsored Israel were sincere. They wanted a home for the homeless Jews of the world, but in trying to solve one problem, and doing so in utter violation of the rights of others, they created a problem far bigger than the original one.

The Arabs, obviously heartsick at their betrayal by the UN, decided to ignore the partition decree. Then followed bitter fighting, the eventual recognition of the new state of Israel by Russia and the United States, and the problem of the Palestinian refugees.

Having learned something about the birth of Israel, I was anxious to know more about Zionism and Judaism. I submitted a list of questions to Rabbi Elmer Berger, executive vice-president of the American Council for Judaism in New York City. This organization says it is

founded on the basic proposition that Judaism is a religion of universal values—not a nationality. We seek for Americans of Jewish faith their increasing civic, cultural and social integration into U.S. life. The Council's active program enables American Jews to meet obligations in public affairs, religion and philanthropy in ways compatible with our beliefs rather than in the "Jewish" nationalist pattern of Zionism. The Council affirms that nationality and religion are separate and distinct; that no Jew or group of Jews can speak for all American

Jews; that Israel is the "homeland" of its own citizens only, and not of all Jews.

These are the questions and the verbatim answers given to me by Rabbi Berger:

(Q) What is the difference between Judaism and Zionism?

(A) Judaism is a historic religion. Millions of people, nationals and citizens of many nations, worship God within the broad framework of Judaism's essential doctrines of the unity of God and the brotherhood of man. Judaism has several denominations, ranging from orthodoxy to liberal. Zionism is a politico-national movement. It regards all Jews, regardless of their legal nationality and citizenship, as sharing a common "Jewish" nationalism. Zionism has many political parties. It regards the state of Israel as the "homeland" of this "Jewish" nationalism. Since Zionism is a politico-national movement, there are Christian, Jewish, and "non-believing" Zionists.

(Q) Why do Arabs respect Judaism and fear Zionism?

(A) Arabs respect Judaism because—or at least in the degree that—they respect all the three great religions of "the Book." The prophets of Judaism—and Christianity —are revered also by the followers of the Koran. There are Christian Arabs and Moslem Arabs. I believe there are also Arabs of the Jewish faith still living in Arab lands. There is no inconsistency here, since "Arab" is an ethnic-cultural term. Judaism is a religious term. Arabs fear Zionism because, at least in their opinion—generally —its national-political nature, focused today in the state of Israel, represents the danger of encroachments on their own national-political sovereignties and development. Mr. Dulles noted this fear of "expansionist Zionism" when he visited the Middle East in 1953. It was a greater fear to the Arab, he reported, than the fear of communism. More specifically, Arabs fear Zionism because of its declared intention to "ingather the exiles"— to bring to Israel constantly more of the world's Jews. Arab statesmen fear that to the extent this Zionist policy is successful it will lead to demands or actions for more territory by the state of Israel.

(Q) Does the average American of Jewish faith recognize the dangers of Zionism?

(A) Definitely not. Most American Jews believe Zionism is a simple humanitarian, refugee, rehabilitation movement. They have no conception of its political party divisions or of its nationalistic character.

(Q) How can Americans help such organizations as yours to tell the truth about Zionism?

(A) This is a difficult question to answer, for too many Americans regard the question of Zionism vs. anti-Zionism to be an intra-Jewish problem. As a matter of public record, of course, Zionism has forced recognition of itself as a political factor in the public domain of American life. This is what it wanted to do. Americans therefore can help organizations like ours—I would rather say they have a public obligation to help themselves—by:

(a) understanding Zionism as a *public* issue;
(b) understanding anti-Zionism;
(c) realizing that taking sides on these issues is not an invasion of the *religious* rights or sensibilities of a segment of their fellow citizens;
(d) determining which of these approaches is *best for America*. What will be best for the America we all know and love will be best for American Jews— as for all other Americans;

(e) having once made a knowledgeable choice, speaking out their convictions to their fellow citizens, whether Jew or Christian. The very core of the Council is predicated upon the freedom of American life. Therefore we believe the best *American way* to help the Council is to have a good, solid, dignified and knowledgeable public airing of the issues.

(Q) Is there scriptural authority for the present state of Israel?

(A) There is no scriptural authority for the present state of Israel. Even if one believes *literally* in the prophetic Zion of the Old Testament, the present state neither is geographically the Holy Land, or Zion, nor is it spiritually a fulfillment of the Universal, Messianic dream. The scriptural references to Zion were all *spiritual*. They cannot possibly be rationalized or equated to the present political, military, nationalistic Israeli state.

Rabbi Berger's views on the absence of scriptural authority for the present state of Israel were put even more strongly by Rabbi Irving F. Reichert in an address before the Third Annual Conference of the American Council for Judaism in Philadelphia. Rabbi Reichert stated:

The fundamental principle of the American Council for Judaism is that the Jewish people are essentially a religious community whose strongest tie is a common faith and a common religious tradition. The fundamental principle of Zionism is that the Jewish people are a homeless nationality whose normalcy can only be achieved through the establishment of a Jewish political state in Palestine. . . . The whole future of the Jew is

at stake in the conflict between these clashing philos-
ophies. . . . That millennial hope for national restora-
tion, incontestably one of the major aspirations of
historic Judaism, was thoroughly *religious* in its moti-
vations and objectives. It was reared upon Messianic expectations of a deliverer, who, in God's own time, would
redeem Israel from captivity, restore it to its former
country under the rule of a descendant of the House of
David, rebuild the temple and reinstitute the sacrificial
cult with all its priestly trappings. . . . It is a far cry
from that historic conception of a restored Jewish state
to the program and pattern which is being so vocifer-
ously and violently urged today. Why, the blueprints of
modern political Zionism are not even a reasonable fac-
simile of the classic Jewish conceptions and formulas for
the redemption of Palestine. They do not pretend to be.
An exalted Messianism transfigured the one; a secular
nationalism dominates the other. In the old tradition
God was central; in the new the corporate Jewish state is
apotheosized. . . . The old tradition was motivated by
piety; the new propaganda is propelled by politics.

The late president of the American University of Beirut,
Stephen Penrose, emphasized:

It is essential that confusion be avoided between the
secular, modern, political entity called Israel, and the
Spiritual Kingdom which needs no earthly boundaries
of time and space.

Here then were typical comments regarding the state of
Israel. And I found that the great majority of my own
Jewish friends agreed with the views of the American
Council for Judaism. As Americans, they shared the basic

beliefs held by all Americans: freedom of speech and press, separation of Church and State. They felt that Judaism was their religion, while their nationality was American; that the nationalism of Israel should be kept outside the institutions of American Jews. They stood ready to give a helping hand to Jews in trouble anywhere in the world, including people in the state of Israel. But they wanted to stress, to the public in general, that no Jew or group of Jews can speak for all the Jews in America.

The American Council for Judaism reports that "the total number of actual, enrolled members of Zionist organizations in this country came to less than 650,000 as of 1952 figures"—a small minority of the 5,000,000 Jews in the United States. That this minority may claim that its activities, in the establishment of the state of Israel, represent the best interests of all American Jews, let alone the American public as a whole, must be seriously questioned. As it affects our relations with the Middle East, Zionism is certainly one force requiring further examination and re-evaluation by American citizens of all religions and convictions.

The other major forces urgently requiring our attention if we are to arrive at a clearer understanding of the situation in the Middle East are communism and Arab nationalism.

In November, 1956, shortly after the invasion of Egypt, I spent several days in Beirut, Lebanon, during the meeting of the Arab leaders. I had occasion to talk briefly with King Saud, King Hussein of Jordan, and President Chamoun of Lebanon. During my conversations with Arab leaders and diplomats and with people in the various Arab states, I could not find one voice raised in defense of the Soviet Union and its policies. During this same period doubt was being expressed in the American press about

King Saud's friendship for the United States. He was, in fact, being labeled pro-Nasser and pro-communist by some sources. To anyone thoroughly familiar with the situation, this was a ridiculous charge. The record supporting King Saud's anti-communist feelings was this:

(1) As in all Arab states, the communist party was outlawed in Saudi Arabia.
(2) In 1956 the Soviet Ambassador during a visit to Teheran offered Saud Soviet-bloc arms, similar to those given Egypt and Syria. Saud rejected the proposal.
(3) When Nasser recognized Communist China, Saud refused to do the same. He allowed Nationalist China to open a consulate in Jiddah.
(4) Saud has repeatedly rejected Soviet feelers toward reopening diplomatic relations cut by his father in the 1930s. Saud does not permit commercial representation by any Iron Curtain country in Saudi Arabia.

"Saud is a man who does not compromise with evil," said one of the king's closest advisers. "As a religious leader and guardian of the Holy Places, he regards communism as pure evil. He doesn't believe you can compromise with evil by trade or by diplomacy."

This pattern of anticommunism was quite evident throughout the Arab world, *despite* the propaganda machine which wished to equate Arab nationalism with communism. I reported in the *Los Angeles Times* on January 1, 1957:

Among Arabs everywhere, in Saudi Arabia, Iraq, Lebanon, Jordan, I found deep resentment over Russian actions in Hungary and Poland. Arab leaders realize as never before that communism and Islam have nothing in common. Islam is a deeply religious faith. Communism is a Godless philosophy.

One Arab leader had said to me on this trip: "There is too much in Christianity and Islam which brings us together for anything like communism to separate us."

I had asked this question of virtually every leader and diplomat in the Arab world: "What is your opinion of communism?" And the answers were almost word for word the same as that given to me by Moussa Shabandar, Iraqi ambassador to the U.S.: "Communism presents a threat to all the free world, including the Arab world."

Following the invasion of Egypt by Israel, France, and Great Britain, the Soviet Union, of course, won a tremendous psychological victory in the Arab world. The prompt action of President Eisenhower to condemn aggression, no matter who the aggressor was, won many friends for the United States in the Middle East. But later action, or rather inaction, by the United States lost us much of this friendship.

What does Arab nationalism promise to the average Arab? Salah Bitar, former foreign minister of Syria, expressed great confidence:

The Arab world will become within this time [10 to 15 years] one Arab homeland . . . in which all Arabs believe and for the realization of which they strive today. The Arab in Kuwait, or Sudan, or Saudi Arabia . . . does not differ from Arabs everywhere in wanting to set up an Arab structure capable, from the political, economic and social points of view, of filling the vacuum left by fragmentation. The Arab, along with his desire for survival, wants to carry the Arab nation to the level of other nations.

This concept of Arab unity was originally urged over seventy-five years ago by students at the American University of Beirut, as the response of young Arab intellectuals to the whole new world of ideas opened up by the introduction of American education. The enthusiasm for Arab unity which first arose within the halls of the American University soon swept through the entire Middle East in an awakening of political consciousness in which Islam became a further source of inspiration and a powerful motivating force.

A group of young Arab students studying at the University of California at Los Angeles had interesting answers to questions on Arab nationalism which I had posed to them in my home in Pacific Palisades. Hisham Nazer is a Saudi Arab, twenty-two years old, who recently obtained his master's degree in international law. He has since returned to work in the Saudi Arabian government. Here are his views:

(Q) Is it in the best interests of America to support Arab nationalism?

(A) Definitely, since it is in the best interests of America to support progressive forces everywhere; and Arab nationalism is a progressive force. It has been striving to raise the standard of living of the Arab peoples, to increase education, to give the people a sense of dignity which they have lost over the past fifty years or so under colonial rule and the Ottoman Empire. America supports progressives in the Philippines and other areas of the world and certainly would do well to support Arab nationalism in the same way, for the same reasons.

(Q) What is your opinion of Gamel Abdel Nasser?

(A) Let me quote Nasser's own opinion of himself.

He wrote: "The annals of history are full of heroes who carved for themselves great and heroic roles, and played them on momentous occasions. It seems to me that in the Arab world there is a role wandering in search of a hero." I believe that he was stating the matter accurately, and that he was, in fact, volunteering to fill this important role when he began his rise to power.

(Q) Is Nasser a dictator?

(A) There has never been a democracy in the Middle East in the Western sense, since democracy is a system of government by the people which can develop only where there are already adequate facilities for educating and informing the people. Until such time as the Arab world enjoys such facilities, a leader like Nasser will have to serve in the capacity of what you would call a dictator.

Moustapha Akkad is twenty-five, has been studying motion picture production at UCLA, and will return to Damascus, his home town, to work in the Ministry of Communications. I asked him:

(Q) Do you believe Nasser is a force for good in the Arab world?

(A) For the most part, he has been. I do not believe in worshiping people. If Nasser were assassinated we would still have our nationalism, our concept of unity. At the moment, Nasser represents these things to the Arab world.

(Q) Should America have supported Nasser?

(A) The biggest mistake America has made in the eyes of the Arab world was not to support him.

(Q) What do you think of the government of Saudi Arabia?

(A) All the monarchies of the Middle East must eventually disappear. The Arab world will be united into one state.

(Q) Do you think communism is a danger to the Arab world?

(A) It is a great danger. Unfortunately, some Arabs do not realize this. They think there is a difference between the Soviet Union and communism and that, since Russia has been supporting the Arab cause, we must feel friendly to the country, perhaps without even questioning its ideology or form of government. Such ignorance on the part of many Arabs obviously leaves them vulnerable to communist propaganda. Remember, too, that the Arab world has never suffered under communism, but it vividly recalls the colonial domination of the British, French and Turks.

Adnan Shocair is studying horticulture at the University of California at Los Angeles. He will return to his native Jordan to work in the government. He is twenty-five.

(Q) What about people who say Arab nationalism is a dangerous force, which could be turned against us?

(A) Nationalism is not an aggressive movement against any other country. It is the will to govern ourselves rather than have our policy dictated, as in the past, by the British or the French. Nationalism is an expression of resistance to imperialism, to communism, to anything that seeks to subjugate or disunite Arabs. Communism is the diametric opposite of nationalism, and there is no possibility of reconciling two such conflicting forces. Our aim is not conquest or domination of other nations, but unification and development of our own people into one nation.

Mahmoud Sherif is twenty-nine, comes from Cairo, and is studying television production. He plans to work in the Ministry of Communications in Egypt.

(Q) If Arab nationalism is not an aggressive movement, why are Nasser's speeches to the people characterized by violence?

(A) In the illiterate Middle East, a rousing call to arms is far more readily understandable than the sort of political subtleties which can be presented to educated, informed American voters at election time. If Nasser abandoned the language of the people—before they have had an opportunity to learn any other language—the people would abandon him. For Nasser to adopt a more restrained approach now, an approach more acceptable to the Western powers, might cost him his leadership— at the very time when the people need such leadership, in just this form, in order to focus their energies on the objectives of unification and internal reform.

(Q) How do you answer charges of friendliness toward communism?

(A) Those of us who understand it hate communism. But we accepted aid from the Russians—after you had refused to help us; and we cannot help liking the people who aided us when we were in trouble. During World War II you joined forces with the Russians. You regarded them as your allies. To the average Arab, it seems about the same thing if, in our own crisis, we regard them as our friends. Nasser, in time of need, has been quick to call on Russian help—in the belief that he can use it without being used. The fact remains that the aims and ideals of Arab nationalism must be forever incompatible with communism, and the success of the nationalist movement is our surest guarantee against the encroachment of communism upon the Arab world.

Perhaps the most forthright summation of the matter was offered by Lebanese businessman Emile Bustani, in his recent book *Doubts and Dynamite:*

The majority of Arab countries would infinitely rather accept Western cooperation than Russian aid. The only essential is that such cooperation should be proffered as between equals, in genuine friendship. What is known as gunboat diplomacy can never quell or even weaken the spirit of nationalism. One does not expect the West to come to the Middle East cap in hand, but the Middle East will never again accept it if it comes with the traditional "big stick" in hand. The Arab world and the Western world can cooperate on equal terms to their mutual advantage. Cooperation between them on unequal terms is no longer acceptable, and hence [is] impracticable. Western statesmen must realize that Arabs have come to political maturity.

♙...*12*

The Arab Refugees

On September 16, 1948, the day before his assassination by the Israeli terrorist Stern gang, the late Count Folke Bernadotte, United Nations mediator in Palestine, dispatched his last progress report to the Secretary-General for transmission to the members of the United Nations. Among his seven basic premises for a just peace in Palestine, Count Bernadotte listed the "Right of Repatriation":

The right of innocent people, uprooted from their homes by the present terror and ravages of war, to return to their homes, should be affirmed and made effective, with assurance of adequate compensation for the property of those who may choose not to return.

Despite the adoption of this basic premise by the General Assembly of the UN in its resolution of December 11, 1948, the Palestine Arab refugees remain homeless and uncompensated. They live today in squalor and suffering, growing more suspicious and hostile every day, firm in their belief that America and the West are responsible for the loss of their homes, their farms, their businesses.

I first became conscious of the Palestinian refugees when I met a number of them who had been absorbed by the Saudi Arabian government. I found them generally an intelligent, likable people, above average in education and aware of the political forces which were sweeping across the Middle East. I heard so many stories about the plight of the Palestinians, some of them harrowing and incredible, that I felt I must see for myself what most authorities on the Middle East called "the number-one problem" facing the free world.

We drove for about ten minutes outside the busy city of Beirut until we reached a narrow, winding road which took us toward the outskirts of the refugee camp. We climbed up a rock-strewn road filled with holes and bounded on both sides by crudely constructed huts made of paper, mud, and assorted debris. This was an Arab refugee camp.

A few worn tents were sprawled on the rocky hillside, and a number of Arab children stood alongside the road, staring at us as our car moved slowly up the street. Some of the children's faces were covered with sores and scabs. Women sat beside their tents or huts, glancing at us with no show of emotion.

An old Palestinian passed us on the road on his donkey, his gray beard heavy with dirt, his eyes staring straight

(*above*) King Saud cuts the ribbon at official opening of the Dammam Primary School, December 7, 1957. (*below*) Camels, near a well in background, in Mukalla, principal port of the Hadhramaut region of the Quaiti State near the southern border of Saudi Arabia, where camel caravans form for journeys to other parts of the Arabian peninsula.

Tens of thousands of Arabs pray at dawn in the Saudi Arabian capital, Riyadh, in the presence of King Saud, at the celebration of the feast which ends Ramadhan. Ramadhan is the Moslem month of fasting.

Waagenaar—Pix

Bedouin camel herders bring their camels to the Aramco-built water trough at Jauf, Eastern Province, Saudi Arabia. Tents belong to the Bedouins.

Arabian American Oil Company

Tarish ibn Hashim Za-
wawi, a young boy living
in Jiddah, Saudi Arabia,
with a cluster of dates
given to him on his visit
to a date garden on the
Mecca Road.

Water sellers still dis-
pense fresh water from
their camel-drawn carts
in some ancient cities of
the Arabian peninsula.

Arabian American Oil Company

(*above*) Blanche and Sam Myers, long-time residents of Saudi Arabia, first Americans to grow grass in Ras Tanura. (*left*) Khalifa ibn Ahmad, a head operator at the Aramco refinery at Ras Tanura, takes son Ibrahim on a tour. (*below*) Author with his driver, Atiyah bin Ibrahim, at Dhahran Airport.

ahead, unseeing and unfriendly. An old woman, perhaps in her seventies, wearing a faded black dress, sat cross-legged in front of a tent. We stopped the car and I greeted her in Arabic. She glared at me, then turned away and spat on the ground. Her face was a sickly yellow, and her hair was matted with dirt.

We drove further up the road into the heart of the camp. Young Palestinians worked alongside the road putting up a barbed-wire fence. We stopped again, and my interpreter and I talked to several of the boys.

"How long have you been here?" I asked one boy of fifteen, a thin, dark-haired Palestinian with bright blue eyes.

"Two years," he answered.

"Before that?"

"Jordan. Palestine." He shrugged his shoulders. "Any place we could find a home."

"Is there work here for you?" I asked.

"No work," he answered. He asked if I was American. Then he began to talk in staccato bursts.

"When will America help us regain our homes? Our farms? When will you stop the Israelis? When will you practice justice with us? That is all we ask—justice!" The boy's face was tense, his voice charged with emotion.

Several of the boys led us on a tour of the huts and tents. As many as eight and ten people were living in tents designed for four people. The huts were almost beyond description, and the smell of human excrement mixed with stale cooking permeated the air. There were newspaper pictures of Nasser on the walls of some huts.

Farther along the road we stopped in front of one of the larger huts. It belonged to a man who was considered a spokesman for the refugees. A sign over the door of the hut read: "Amin b'Allah." We stopped and talked to the man, a tall, thin, middle-aged Arab with gray hair, kindly eyes, and a gentle smile. I asked him what the sign meant.

"It means, 'In God I have faith,' " he answered. "That is all we have left . . . faith."

I learned that the man had lost a profitable business in Palestine, a good home, and two of his children in the fighting. I asked him what America could do to help solve the refugee problem.

"We have been here for eight years," he said. "We were forced to leave our homes, but we thought it was only for a short time. But now we are losing hope . . . even our faith in God. Your country must stand up for justice, must help us to regain our homes and our land."

I talked with several other well-educated Arabs that day, and all said basically the same thing: we cannot understand the Jewish claim to Palestine. How can they claim a country just because they lived in it two thousand years ago? Is it right for them to claim they are the chosen people of God? Are we not all children of God? Has one religion the right to take over the Holy Land that is the rightful property of Christians and Moslems as well? How long will America allow Zionists to create hatred between the Jews and Arabs who had been living for centuries in peace? Was it just for the Zionists to create a country of their own at the expense of a million Arabs? Was this justice? Was it the will of God?

Several small Arab boys ran alongside the car as we left the camp that afternoon, handsome boys, their faces wreathed in smiles. They wanted *baksheesh*. The younger children, I thought, still trusted strangers, still looked for friendship. An attractive Palestinian girl of fourteen or fifteen stood in the doorway of a tent watching us. She was dressed in a plain, faded robe. Her dark hair was brushed smooth. Her brown eyes were wistful. She had been only a small child at the time of her people's betrayal. Eight years of cruel hardship and injustice had perhaps all but destroyed many of the first-generation refugees. But these youngsters could still grow up unscarred, if amends were made in time.

The extent of the injustice, about which there is no general agreement, can be understood only by considering the many widely varied views and opinions on the situation. I have discussed it with Zionists as well as the refugees themselves; with UNRWA officials and American relief representatives. I have studied the documents of the United Nations and of the Arab and Israeli governments. The salient features of the case seem to me to be as follows:

(1) The Israelis say there would be no refugee problem if the Arabs had accepted the partition plan in 1947 and had not attacked Israel.

(2) The Arabs maintain that they were forcibly driven out by the Israelis. They say that even before the partition plan, many thousands of Jewish refugees had already been brought into Palestine, many illegally, causing mounting fear among the Arabs who had made their homes there for generations, centuries. The Arabs then placed their hopes in the UN for a solution to this problem—only to be presented with a partition plan requiring that the larger and more fertile part of Palestine go to the Jews. This, the Arabs would not accept. Even before the Arabs attacked the Jews in protest against partition, Jewish terrorist groups had begun attacking Arab villages to induce the Arabs to leave the country. Then Jewish extremists wiped out whole Arab villages, men, women and children, as in the Deir Yassin massacre, frightening thousands more Arabs out of the area.

(3) By the time the Arab-Israeli war started officially, after the withdrawal of British troops, nearly 300,000 Arabs had already taken refuge. British loudspeaker trucks drove

through the streets of the cities telling the Arab population, in Arabic, to leave. After the start of the war, another 600,000 refugees followed suit.

If the blame is difficult to fix, it is also difficult to say who is free of blame. The British, who left the area in chaos? The Jews, who were determined to create their own state, Israel, in an area they knew was hostile to them? The Arab leaders, or politicians, who used the refugees for political ends? The United States, under President Harry S. Truman, who participated with the UN in the creation of the state of Israel? . . . Mankind in general?

President Truman must have felt this responsibility when he wrote, in his 1951 report to Congress: "Until this large body of uprooted and homeless people find new homes and economic opportunities, they will constitute a potentially destructive force in this vitally important area of the world."

Today the nearly one million Arab refugees live in conditions almost beyond description in the Arab states, the majority of them, over half a million, in Jordan. The next largest group, about 220,000, are in the Gaza Strip. This means that four fifths of all the refugees live in two areas which are unable to feed them or provide them with work. Of the 930,000 registered with UNRWA, 840,000 are on the relief rolls of the United Nations. They receive approximately seven cents a day on which to exist. They receive a diet of 1,600 calories daily in winter and 1,500 in summer. Although most of the refugees receive relief from UNRWA, only 360,000 live in camps.

The refugee camps vary from about 800 people to cities of over 30,000. Most of the early accommodations consisted of small tents designed to shelter three to five people, but which actually housed as many as ten. Refugees have rioted against the building of improved shelters, since they take this to mean there is no chance of their returning to their old homes and farms.

Terrible as the conditions are in many of the camps—crowded living quarters, lack of privacy, idleness and poverty—there is surprisingly little crime or immorality. The refugees in many camps manage to keep clean and to maintain their personal dignity and hospitality despite the years which have brought only futility and despair.

The opinion of many interested groups and individuals is that these long years of hopeless waiting might have been ended at any time by one responsible gesture from Israel —some effort, however inadequate, in behalf of the refugees.

Yet, in discussing the refugee problem with Zionists, I find the majority of them honestly convinced that the state of Israel has no responsibility to the Arab refugees, since they were openly urged by their own leaders to flee their lands and homes during the fighting. The conditions prompting the Arabs' flight must be understood before this argument can be evaluated.

Dr. Stephen Penrose, then president of the American University of Beirut, wrote in his *Minaret* pamphlet:

On both sides dreadful deeds were committed, but, in the main, the Zionists made better use of the terrorist tactics which they learned only too well at the hands of Nazi taskmasters. There is no question but that frightful massacres such as that which took place at Deir Yassin in April, 1948, were perpetrated for the major purpose of frightening the Arab population and causing them to take flight. The Zionist radio repeated incessantly for the benefit of Arab listeners, "Remember Deir Yassin." Terror is contagious, and it built up the tre-

mendous migration leading to the results which may
be witnessed in the refugee camps.

The massacre is described by Erich W. Bethmann in his
Minaret pamphlet:

> The Irgun and the Stern Groups were assigned to look
> after Deir Yassin. When they ran into trouble, they asked
> Haganah for help. With its help the village was oc-
> cupied. After the Haganah men had withdrawn, mem-
> bers of the Irgun and Stern Group perpetrated the most
> revolting atrocities: 254 Arab men, women and children
> were butchered in cold blood and their mutilated bodies
> thrown into a well; captured Arab women and girls were
> paraded through the streets of the Jewish quarter in
> Jerusalem. Deir Yassin will never be forgotten by the
> Arabs. It had an important secondary result: it struck
> panic into the hearts of the Arab villagers, and a large-
> scale exodus began. . . .

Rabbi Elmer Berger wrote a number of moving and en-
lightening letters during his visit to the Middle East in
1955. Later these letters were incorporated into a book,
Who Knows Better Must Say So. Of the Arab refugees,
Rabbi Berger wrote:

> You can imagine the very great emotional disturbance I
> have experienced these past few days. It was compounded
> by my first visit to an Arab refugee camp. . . . The
> worst living conditions are in caves, and some of the
> tent camps are only slightly better. Here human beings
> live like animals . . . disintegrating mentally and mor-
> ally. I have seen the camps in Germany where Jews

lived. These Arab refugee camps are no better—and in some places they are worse.

The historian Arnold Toynbee wrote in Volume VIII of his *A Study of History:*

> The Jews' immediate reaction to their own experience was to become persecutors in their turn . . . at the first opportunity that had risen for them to inflict on other human beings, who had done the Jews no injury, but happened to be weaker than they were, some of the wrongs and sufferings that had been inflicted on the Jews by their many successive Western Gentile persecutors during the intervening seventeen centuries. . . . The Arabs in Palestine . . . became in their turn the vicarious victims of the European Jews' indignation over the genocide committed upon them by their Gentile fellow Westerners in A.D. 1933-45.

Professor Toynbee, no anti-Semite, made it clear that this tragic phenomenon of persecuted turned persecutors was by no means unique with the Jews, but was, on the contrary, characteristic of all mankind. All mankind must hope, then, that the phenomenon will stop with these last innocent victims, the Arab refugees.

It thus becomes the urgent duty of us all to seek the solution to this grievous—and dangerous—problem in the Middle East. Certainly it will not be solved by David Ben Gurion and other Zionist leaders saying in effect: the Arab refugees are not the type of people we want in Israel.

Nor will the problem be solved by a truculent attitude on the part of some Arab diplomats. There must be a lessening of the bitterness and hatred on both sides.

More Americans are coming to realize that our policies
of preference for Israel and our failure to face the realities
of the Arab refugees have cost us many friends throughout
the world. As a nation, we have suffered a loss of prestige.
As individuals, none of us was directly responsible for the
perpetration of this injustice; our failure—which it is not
too late to correct—has been ignorance, lack of understanding.

In my lecture work I have ample opportunity to observe
how eager and grateful the average American citizen is for
a chance to learn the truth, and thus to assume his individual share of the responsibility for this situation, which
represents a challenge to all mankind. Great numbers of
men and women in my audiences were quick to respond
once they learned about the plight of the Arab refugees.
They found time to inform others of the problem and
joined organizations endeavoring to help the refugees.
When I displayed dolls and other items made by the refugees in their camps, refugee headquarters were invariably
overwhelmed by letters from people who wanted to pur-
chase these items and thus, in some small way, help individual refugees feel like productive members of society.

Even Zionists frequently approached me after my talks
to express their appreciation for my "fair, objective treatment of Middle East problems." But other Zionists opposed me angrily, branding me "anti-Semitic" and an
"Arab propagandist." Their often discourteous, intemper-
ate efforts to discredit me, while these were trying to me
personally and for others concerned with my lecture work,
as well as for my audiences, inevitably succeeded only in
making enemies for Israel. Americans do not like unwarranted criticism, nor do they uphold those who seek to
threaten others into silence with a carelessly tossed epithet
or insult. My own remarks from the platform, never hostile

to Israel or Zionism but only encouraging to greater understanding of both the Arab and the Israeli and of the special
problems of the Arab refugees, could not possibly have
aroused antipathy toward the state of Israel.

I asked Elmer Berger what the official position of the
American Council for Judaism was, regarding the Arab
refugees. Did it offer a solution? He answered:

> The Council takes no official position on this problem.
> We have, through our Philanthropic Fund, contributed
> to some relief projects for the refugees. Personally, I
> subscribe largely to the opinions of the Honorable
> Henry R. Labouisse, former chief of the UNRWA. I
> believe Israel must recognize the *principle* of repatria-
> tion. It would, I believe, in view of the Arab-Israel con-
> flict, be entitled to exact from any who might seek re-
> patriation, binding oaths of loyalty in return for which
> Israel would be expected to end the disabilities its Arab
> population now endures. For those who, finding Israel
> of today different from the Palestine they left a decade
> ago, decided against repatriation, adequate compensa-
> tion must be provided. This basic formula, plus minor
> concessions in the present "boundaries," plus plans for
> regional economic development, would probably pro-
> vide solutions for a major part of the refugees.

Per-Olow Anderson, in his photo-essay on the Palestine
Arab refugees, entitled, "They Are Human Too," states:
"I seek to show by these pictures how like these men,
women and children are to our parents, our brothers and
sisters, and our neighbors." Mr. Anderson's book will
evoke in any reader a deeper concern for human suffering
and a recognition that human dignity must be restored to
the Palestine refugees. At the opening of his book, Mr.

Anderson has quoted the following words of Woodrow Wilson:

> Justice has nothing to do with expediency. Justice has nothing to do with any temporary standard whatever. It is rooted and grounded in the fundamental instincts of Humanity.

🐫...*13*

A Decade of Change

It was 118 degrees the afternoon I arrived in Saudi Arabia
in the summer of 1959. I had time for a quick trip to
Dhahran and Jiddah and Riyadh, to see the continuing
changes taking place in the desert kingdom of King Saud.
As always there was the perpetual glare of gas flares from
the oil fields, the camel trains weaving across the desert,
the veiled women, and the Bedouin.

But now there were also Arabs becoming millionaires
overnight, modern communities rising on the edge of the
desert with neon signs announcing their birth. And everywhere Arabs were beholding with their very eyes marvels

of modern ingenuity to dazzle the imagination and set them dreaming of a new kind of life for themselves: for television had come to Saudi Arabia!

Aramco had opened a TV station in 1957 on an experimental basis, to run two hours a day. It was intended primarily for the company's Saudi Arabian employees. So popular did the station become that it now operates approximately four hours daily with Arabic programs. Since there are no motion-picture theaters, night clubs, or other forms of public entertainment for Saudi Arabs, Aramco's TV station was an oasis in an entertainment desert. Sales of TV sets boomed within a hundred-mile range.

In talking with Saudi Arabian officials during this trip, I found increasing awareness of the many problems which faced the Arab world. "Certainly Arab nationalism is a vital force in the Middle East today," one Saudi Arabian minister told me. "There is a new sense of dignity among Arabs, a realization that the poverty in our countries must be met by intelligent use of the oil money."

Many Saudi Arabs in all walks of life told me President Nasser was still highly regarded as a leader, although not so much so as many Saudi Arabs had considered him originally. Young King Hussein's prestige had slipped among the more intelligent Arabs. "Hussein is a courageous young man," one Saudi Arabian member of the royal family told me, "but he does not represent the will of the people, and this will be his undoing."

During those weeks in the Arab world when I had occasion to visit with King Saud, King Hussein, and President Nasser, I became convinced more than ever that Nasser, while the symbol of Arab nationalism at the present time, is only the effect of Arab nationalism, not its cause, and that if Nasser were to be eliminated tomorrow there would be a new Arab symbol of nationalism to take his place the next day. This fact seems to have escaped the anti-Nasserites among the British, French, and Israelis.

It had become popular in America to support King Hussein and to oppose President Nasser. This was understandable because of his friendship to the West. King Hussein, by his friendly attitude, was receiving American aid in the amount of twenty million dollars a year. But it was common knowledge in the Middle East that the king's government was one of the least stable and perhaps the most unpopular.

"By your support of Hussein, may you not be postponing the day when the turmoil and instability in the Arab world can be replaced by something based on mutual trust and understanding?" one Jordanian newspaperman asked me in Amman.

Here again Arab nationalism was the focal point at issue, and King Hussein to most Arabs is the antithesis of Arab nationalism. I had this brought forcibly to my attention in the spring of 1959 when I spoke to the Fourth Regional Arab Students' Convention in Los Angeles. More than three hundred Arab students representing fourteen nations were in attendance.

The night before my scheduled talk I heard King Hussein address the Los Angeles World Affairs Council. I spent the remainder of the evening at an Arabian Nights celebration held as part of the students' convention. I found much bitterness among the Arab students over the king's appearance in Los Angeles. Many wanted to picket the king during his stay. I made my feelings quite clear that night to some of the Arab officers: I did not wish to address the convention the following night if anything was done to embarrass the youthful monarch. I felt the students would only discredit themselves and their cause by such action.

Fortunately, cooler heads prevailed, and the next morning the students met with King Hussein in a rather heated session in his suite at the Ambassador Hotel. As an aftermath of this meeting, Mustapha Akaad, chairman of the convention, a handsome young Syrian, wrote an open letter to the king. Parts of it seemed to be extremely well put. He wrote:

> We haven't learned anything new from your answers except that you are separated from your people. You are surrounded by opportunists who are blinding your eyes from the facts about the Arab world and especially the Arabs of Jordan. . . . In one of your statements you said, "I want to maintain Jordan." Do you think that Jordan can maintain herself economically or are you depending upon sterling and dollars and for how long? I think you know that the future of the Arab world is in Arab nationalism and unity. The more you delay this unity, the more you are betraying the Arab people. Why don't you follow the example of Shukry Al-Kuwatly [Syrian president], who, after being a president of an independent, self-supporting state and loved by the people, sacrificed his presidency for the unity of the Arabs. . . . His name will be mentioned with the greats of our history. Your Majesty, if you neglected during your tour of the United States to mention anything about Algeria and Palestine with which you are directly involved, then where does your statement stand, "I am willing to give my life to the Arab cause"? We don't want you to give up your life, just your throne, and give the people of Jordan the freedom to decide their destiny by a free plebiscite.
>
> Your Majesty, a throne in the hearts of the people is better than a thousand thrones with the force of guns

and jails. Arab unity has to come because it is the wish of the people; we believe only in the ideology of Arab nationalism and respect the men who serve it. Leaders come and go, but Arab nationalism and unity remain.

It was in the last part of this young Syrian's letter to King Hussein that I believe he touched on the crux of the situation. Indeed, it makes little difference today who the leaders are so long as they support Arab nationalism. This accounts in part for Nasser's initial willingness to go along with General Kassem of Iraq, as long as the latter indicated his awareness of the communist danger.

There were encouraging signs that Americans were awakening to the necessity of understanding the Arabs and, by the same reasoning, were having serious doubts about the continual Zionist claims that President Nasser was another Hitler, the real bogey man behind all the troubles of the Middle East.

When I was speaking at a conference of teachers in the summer of 1959, a woman came up to me with a copy of Abba Eban's *The Tide of Nationalism* in her hands. "How could this obviously intelligent spokesman for the Israelis expect us to swallow this bunk about Arab nationalism?" she said quite heatedly. "He must think we are all ignorant of the Arabs and their real feelings."

I had not read this lecture by the former Israeli ambassador to the United States, but I had heard Eban speak not many months before in Los Angeles. He spent considerable time assuring the audience that Nasser was behind all the trouble in Iraq and that the menace of communism in that area was greatly exaggerated . . . this despite the warning a week previous from Allen Dulles of the Central Intelligence Agency that the communist threat was nowhere more evident than in Iraq.

After reading Eban's lecture, in which he compares Nasser to Hitler, debunks the theory of Arab unity and nationalism, and indicates that Nasser is evil and is more resented and feared than honored in the Arab world, I could not wonder that an increasing number of Americans were resenting the obvious Israeli propaganda in America to discredit the Arabs, their leaders, and even Americans who tried to tell the truth about the Arabs.

(It reminded me of the best-selling novel *Exodus*, labeled as Zionist propaganda by reviewers of *Time, The Christian Science Monitor,* and other wide-awake publications. In *Exodus,* Arabs are backward, fanatical, savage, dirty, and illiterate.)

Eban surely knows that anyone who has visited the Arab capitals of the Middle East, talked to the people in the streets, the leaders, the diplomats, the uneducated and the educated would admit that Nasser is the symbol of Arab nationalism, a dynamic force which does exist in the Arab world, and that the dream of Arabs everywhere is for one united Arab state. Whether Nasser himself becomes that leader is secondary to the hopes of most Arabs.

When Eban criticizes Nasser for his lack of social reforms, when he says quite seriously that Arab hostility to the West has nothing to do with Arab-Israeli relations, he obviously is trying to make us believe that black is white. Nasser's social projects and reforms may have amounted to less than had been expected, but he has made progress in Egypt. Any student of Middle East affairs could not help but conclude from all the facts available that the creation of the state of Israel has had much to do with Arab feelings toward the West.

When I was in Cairo, Amin Shaikr, personal secretary to President Nasser, showed me a file one afternoon which contained an article written by an American. The article appeared in one of the large Sunday newspaper supplements and was supposedly an exclusive interview with President Nasser at his home. The writer described Nasser as a diabetic and said he did not marry his wife for love and was in general a very dangerous man. Shaikr was upset when he told me: "This man came to Cairo, asked for an interview with the president, and when it could not be granted, went back to America after one week and wrote this nonsense without having ever seen the President."

With this background in mind, perhaps it is not difficult to understand why so much anti-Nasser opinion exists in America today. Nasser is anti-Western, anti-Israeli, critics say. We cannot maintain profitable relations with him. Yet King Hussein is just as anti-Israeli as Nasser, and so are King Saud and Prince Faisal, but we have friendly and profitable relations with Saudi Arabia.

Nasser is accused of wanting to grab all the Arab states and put them under his leadership. While I could not ask this question of Nasser directly, I did put it to a man who has been one of his closest friends. He replied, "The president is only concerned with a loose federation of Arab states in which Egyptian leadership, not dictatorship, is secured."

In saying that Nasser is anti-Western we forget that this is true only to the extent that he wants no Western control over Arab policy. But he also wants no Soviet control; he abhors it and fights it. He does business with the Soviets and would do so with us, as he points out, if he could be convinced there were no strings attached.

When Abba Eban was telling Americans there was no communist danger in Iraq, Nasser was telling an Indian journalist in Cairo:

I can tell you we had reliable information of a communist master plot to seize Iraq and to establish a Soviet state in this strategic Arab region, then to cause a split between Syria and Egypt and break up our union; then to proceed to the ultimate communist goal of creating a Red Fertile Crescent, that is, a federation formed of Iraq, Syria, Jordan, Lebanon, and Kuwait, perhaps to provide the Soviet Union with access not only to the Persian Gulf and the Gulf of Aqaba, but the Indian Ocean as well. . . .

Would support of Nasser help to defeat communism in the Middle East? I asked this question of people in every Arab country. An emphatic "yes" was the answer that most qualified observers gave me. One need only visit Iraq and talk to the Iraqis to understand why. General Kassem and his immediate advisers have learned about the dangerous nature of Soviet communism. They have learned it the hard way and perhaps too late.

I remembered what one Egyptian minister told me, a man obviously friendly to America: "Communism poses a real danger to the Arab world. Your support of President Nasser, despite the objections of Israel which fears him, would insure the defeat of communism in the Arab world."

I thought of these statements on my return flight to the United States that summer. I felt encouraged by what I had seen in the Middle East. But I arrived in New York to find considerable adverse publicity being given Aramco by Judge Henry Epstein of the New York State Supreme Court, in connection with the company's alleged practice of "discrimination." The background of the whole affair was very interesting.

Under the rulings of the Saudi government, visas are not

normally granted to Jews. The company knew that under New York State law an applicant's religion or race could not be asked. To avoid direct conflict with the law, Aramco requires applicants who might be sent to Saudi Arabia to apply for a visa to that country. The Saudi Arabian visa application form can and does ask the racial and religious information.

In 1950 the New York State Commission Against Discrimination accepted this arrangement on grounds that the national interest required Aramco to be able to function in Saudi Arabia. The United States State Department had been in favor of such an agreement. Then Judge Epstein overruled the commission, stating that "the discrimination practiced by Aramco in New York State must cease." He then went further and told Aramco to "go elsewhere to serve your Arab master."

The chairman of the State Commission Against Discrimination stated he would appeal, adding, "in matters of national security," the commission would "be guided by statements of the Federal Government as to the best interests of the United States." The State Department's earlier position had been quite clear when it pointed out that any effort to compel Aramco to hire Jews "would most certainly prejudice the company's operations . . . and would probably adversely affect the United States' interests as well."

Reaction to Judge Epstein's decision brought some interesting comment. It awakened many Americans to long-overlooked facts about overseas areas: American Negroes are not permitted in Iceland. Catholic Spain objected to Protestant airmen from America, although officially we did not give in to such Catholic pressure. India has its concept of "untouchability." Norway permits no Jesuits.

Elias N. Koussa of Haifa, Israel, the spokesman for the Arab minority in Israel, writing in the *Jewish Newsletter*, stated:

It is surprising how the American Zionists strongly oppose discrimination by Aramco against the Jews and yet enthusiastically support, or at least acquiesce in, the discrimination exercised by Israel against its Arab citizens. For the last eleven years, these Arabs have been suffering from serious discriminatory practices by the military rule imposed on racial grounds in all areas predominantly inhabited by Arabs . . .

Mr. Koussa went on to point out that the reason given by Israeli and Zionist leaders for imposition of such a rule against the Arabs was one of security. Since a state of war still exists between Saudi Arabia and Israel, Mr. Koussa asks if that is not a stronger justification for the Saudi policy of excluding Jews from employment by Aramco.

Ironically enough, the boycott of which the American Zionists and Israel complain with much ado is a weapon which the Arab learned from the Zionist Jews themselves [Mr. Koussa adds]. It was first invoked during the mandatory regime by the Jewish Agency . . . by nearly every Jewish institution of importance. . . . In these political and commercial organizations it was a rule of procedure that no Arab should be employed. The Jews considered the boycott fully justified and lawful. Now it has become unlawful and undemocratic because it is being used by the Arabs against the Jews. . . .

William Zukerman, editor of the *Jewish Newsletter*, pointed out:

While Saudi Arabia has in effect adopted the full Zionist theory of the unity of all Jews with Israel as its head-quarters, the Zionists and pro-Zionist organizations in America are confusing the issue by ignoring the political and nationalistic causes of the boycott introduced by Israel and presenting it as a case of simple antisemitic discrimination.

Earlier in this book I have given King Saud's reply as to why he does not allow Jews in Saudi Arabia. Right or wrong, he believes he must keep out of his country those people who could constitute a subversive force, and since Israel preaches the doctrine that all Jews, wherever they may live, must support Israel and its policies, it could be concluded that King Saud has justifiable reasons for his decision.

In an editorial on the Aramco case, Zukerman summed up his feelings in the *Jewish Newsletter* as follows:

Peace is a plant that cannot thrive in an atmosphere of arrogance and militancy such as Jewish nationalism has almost deliberately fostered during the last fifteen years . . . We must recognize and admit publicly that justice and truth are not the monopoly of the Jews, that the Arabs, too, have claims just as valid as the Israeli claims, and that not everyone who says so is an antisemite. A change in approach and policy will follow by itself.

Perhaps Zukerman has touched upon the heart of the matter, the necessity for the Zionists to recognize that their cause can never be advanced by the continual tearing down of the Arabs or those who in a spirit of friendship try to present the Arab viewpoint.

Several years ago a Zionist official on the West Coast, in

the course of his duties, complained to a well-known public forum that since I had been booked as a speaker the forum should schedule a speaker on Israel. He claimed I was pro-Arab and anti-Israeli. Several days later I arranged to have lunch with this man, and in a kindly manner I pointed out to him that such behind-the-scenes maneuvering was only hurting the cause which he represented.

As a result of that luncheon we became good friends. Sometime later this gentleman resigned his position in the Zionist organization. I believe that more and more American Zionists are recognizing that the future of Israel will be aided by an attitude of moderation and understanding on the part of those who direct the world-wide Zionist organization.

🐫...*14*

An American Named Sami Hussein

My last visit with Sami Hussein in the summer of 1959 was an experience I shall long remember. I had not seen Sami for nearly five years, although we had kept in touch through correspondence. Wrapped up as I was in my lecture work and the occasional visits to the Middle East, my thoughts of this gentle, kind Saudi Arab had been much too infrequent.

I knew that he had come to New York to work for Aramco, but I did not realize the circumstances under which he had made the trip, nor did I know that he had just recently become an American citizen. It was an exciting story, and I learned the details that first night as I sat with him in his home in Levittown, New York.

Sami had been unhappy after returning to Saudi Arabia from his teaching duties at the Riverhead school. He had become thoroughly "Americanized," as he put it. He had learned to live like an American and think like one, and he found that back in Saudi Arabia his talents were not being used to the fullest.

"I wanted to go to America and live," Sami told me, "to become an American citizen, and then come back some day and help my people. I knew it was an almost impossible dream. No one had ever done it before, but I was determined to make the effort."

Sami went to the American consul in Dhahran and asked, "What must I do to go to America and become a United States citizen?"

The consul was so amazed at the request, the first of its kind ever made, that he had to look up the details himself.

Sami learned there was a quota which allowed one hundred Saudi Arabs to emigrate to the United States each year. The quota had reached eight hundred because no Saudi Arab had emigrated to America since the quota was established. But the requirements for an emigrant gave Sami concern. He must have a sponsor in America, someone who would vouch for him; a police clearance from Saudi officials; and three thousand dollars in cash.

Sami knew he could get the sponsor, and perhaps the police clearance. But the three thousand dollars was a real problem . . . until Aramco made a personnel shift which was to provide an opportunity for Sami to resolve this difficulty. He was sent to the American University of Beirut on a scholarship.

"I became a capitalist in Beirut," Sami told me with a smile. "I bought two taxi cabs and ran them while I went to school. At the end of a year, when I returned to Saudi Arabia, I had my three thousand dollars."

Sami confided his plans to become an American citizen to several of his Aramco friends in Dhahran. They were shocked. "But it's impossible," they told him. "No one has ever done it before."

Eventually, after many weeks of waiting, Sami got a sympathetic ear from "Andy" Anderson, then Aramco's head personnel man. He promised to help, but he warned Sami there were many difficulties involved in such an undertaking. Several months dragged by, and nothing happened. Sami decided he must take matters into his own hands. He went to the American consul and filled out the necessary forms. He obtained his police clearance and bought a one-way ticket for $760 to New York via TWA.

At 5:00 A.M. one morning, Sami awakened in his quarters, dressed quietly so as not to disturb his roommate, packed his bag with only one extra set of underwear, a small toilet kit, a copy of the Koran, and the necessary papers to permit him to emigrate to America. He wore his only suit. His roommate awakened and broke into tears when Sami told him where he was going. "But you will be killed!" his friend cried.

At the airport, the Saudi customs official looked at Sami's passport, his police clearance, his ticket. He was almost too dumbfounded to speak. "Are you sure this is right?" he demanded of Sami. *No one had ever done it before!*

"Of course it's right," Sami said with a pounding heart, knowing that a last-minute telephone call by the official to government headquarters might start him on his way to jail.

For nearly an hour Sami sat in the small, dimly lit waiting room at the Dhahran airport. "It was the longest hour of my life," Sami told me. "The plane was late, and I was

terrified that any minute I would be apprehended by the
Saudi Arabian police. Once my name was called over the
loudspeaker system, and I was too paralyzed to move.
Finally I did answer the call, and it was the TWA representative asking what he could do to help me when I
arrived in New York. I told him: 'Just get me on the plane,
please!' "

Sami arrived in New York after refusing to get off the
plane at Rome; Paris; Shannon, Ireland; or Gander, Newfoundland. "I was afraid I might not get on again," he
said. After clearing with customs and health people in New
York, he went to the YMCA and slept for two days and two
nights. "I had never slept like this before," he told me,
"nor have I since."

For several days Sami walked the streets of New York,
"just looking at America and Americans, the stores, the
cars, realizing how good Allah had been to me." Then he
went to the Aramco office and asked for a job. After several
weeks he became a storekeeper at the Aramco aviation
office at Idlewild Airport. His salary was $230 a month.

Before long he met a Spanish girl at the YWCA. She
spoke no English, he no Spanish. They spoke in sign language. Within a few weeks they fell in love and were
married.

Sami's wife sat across from me this night as he told me
the story. She smiled and occasionally said a few words in
English. Sami now speaks good Spanish, she some Arabic.
They have three daughters. "My biggest thrill is coming
home from work and seeing them in front of the house
waiting for me," Sami said.

I talked with several of Sami's neighbors that evening.
He had been an inspiration to them, the way he worked
on his house. He had added two rooms, beautifully land-
scaped and gardened his lawn. He had put in cement walks

and a new roof. "I believe I have the nicest house in the neighborhood," he told me proudly. "We get a lot of visitors who want to see it."

"Where did you learn to do cement work, roofing, and gardening?" I asked Sami. "I went to night school for a year to learn how to 'raise' the roof," he told me. "I studied books on cement work and watched contractors putting in walks. Then I rented a trailer to pick up rocks and broken cement to use in my walks and garden. I did most of the work on Saturdays, Sundays, and holidays."

Sami enjoyed telling me about the Jewish woman who lived down the street. She came over to look at Sami's garden and said, "If my husband knew I came here, he would divorce me." Sami and the woman became good friends, and eventually she brought her husband to see the garden. He was so impressed with Sami's work that he asked for advice on improving his own yard. Sami ended up doing the gardening for him, because, as he said, "I enjoyed helping one of my neighbors."

Sami showed me his "work room" that night in his home. It was an attractive paneled room on the second floor, crammed with books on the Middle East. In addition to his other labors he had found time to study extensively the problems of the Arab world.

"Do your neighbors ask you questions about the Arabs?" I inquired. Yes, most of them did, Sami told me. They wanted to know why the Middle East was important to America. Why were the Arabs so backward and decadent? "Actually," he admitted, "I didn't have many of the answers. It took me a few weeks of study and research. But then I put together some questions and answers to be used at community meetings I conducted on the Middle East."

I learned that Sami had given a number of talks on Saudi Arabia. He had prepared a very comprehensive list

of questions and answers for members of his audiences. He
had mimeographed the sheets himself, and estimated that
he had given away several thousand. These read in part
as follows:

(Q) How much oil is there in the Middle East?

(A) Between 70% and 90% of the world's known oil
reserves lie in the Arab world. The West controls these
Middle East oil fields, which flow at the rate of more
than 4,000,000 barrels daily to Europe and the world
under concession agreements splitting the profits 50-50
between the companies and the Arab governments. The
total investment of the West in the Middle East is
estimated at about three billion dollars. About fifty
percent of this is American capital.

(Q) Won't atomic power eventually replace oil?

(A) Atomic power can never take the place of crude
oil and its hundreds of uses. The need for Middle East
oil will grow rather than diminish. The economy of
Europe is so dependent on Arab oil that if this oil were
lost to Europe, it would have to rely on the United States
for both oil and dollars. This would eventually inflate
the dollar further and lower the standard of living for
all Americans.

(Q) Does Russia need Middle East oil?

(A) Not at all. But Russia knows what would happen
to Europe and to our economy if she could take Middle
East oil away from us. That is why Russia is making
every effort to divide and conquer the Arab states, to
distort the truth, to fan the flames of discord. Russia
will try to destroy Arab nationalism, although posing as
its champion. It should be remembered that the Czars
were just as anxious to dominate the Middle East as the

communists are today. The Middle East links three continents, Europe, Asia and Africa, and every conqueror in history looked to this area as an important step to conquest.

(Q) Why can't the Arabs and Jews live in peace?

(A) They have for centuries. They have the same historic roots, Abraham fathering both races. Isaac was the son of Abraham and Sarah. Ishmael was the son of Abraham and Hagar the bondwoman. They are of the same blood. The enmity and bitterness between Arab and Jew has come to us as the result of the Zionist insistence upon the creation of the State of Israel on land which had belonged to the Arabs for centuries.

(Q) What have the Arabs ever contributed to world culture?

(A) Unfortunately, most Americans, in looking at the Arab world, at Arabs who need our inspiration, understanding and help in the introduction of modern techniques, see the Arabs only as a limited, backward civilization, people who need a great deal from us but apparently have little or nothing to offer in return. The truth is that the Arab culture in centuries past has contributed much to our present way of life. A highly refined and advanced civilization was flourishing in the Arab world when most of Europe was an intellectual desert and America had never been dreamed of.

Our Western civilization is really an evolution of Arabic cultural achievements which originated during the rise of Islam in the Middle East. We owe a debt of thanks to the Arabs for their contributions in the field of mathematics. They gave us algebra, the zero, the decimal system. Arab contributions to astronomy, geography, medicine, chemistry, agriculture, music and the arts were all vital to further development in these fields. Even in literature we use words like "sugar" from the Arabic "sukr," "cotton" from the Arabic "cutun," and many others. Arabs wrote the first books on paper, and introduced paper to the West from China. Hebrew thinkers lived and worked in the Arab empire when it was at its peak, disproving the falsehood being spread today that Arabs have been anti-Jewish from time immemorial. Great Arab leaders of that period quoted from Jewish sources and authorities with deep respect and gratitude.

(Q) What happened to this Arab culture?

(A) History shows that all civilizations have reached a peak, then declined. In the thirteenth century, at its zenith, the Arab world was overrun by the Mongols. Arab cities, orchards, monuments were razed to the ground. Thousands of people were slaughtered. Then in the fifteenth century the Arabs came under the rule of the Ottoman Turks. This subjugation continued, while Europe advanced culturally. Then came the British and French with colonialism, and it has only been in the past few years that the Arabs have been on their own again to seek unity and dignity and progress.

When I had finished reading several of Sami's mimeographed sheets, he handed me a book from one of the shelves. "Many times people question me at the meetings about my sources of information," he said. "This is one of the best in its detailed discussion of Arab culture."

The book was *Arab Contribution to Civilization* by Rom Landau, Chairman of the Department of Islamic and North African Studies at the College of the Pacific. Sami had marked a quotation by Professor George Sarton of Harvard:

When we try to explain western culture we may leave out almost completely the Hindu and Chinese developments, but we cannot leave out the Arabic one without spoiling the whole story and making it unintelligible. . . . Arabic was the international language of science to a degree which had never been equalled by any other language (except Greek) and has never been repeated since. It was the language not of one people, one nation, one faith, but of many peoples, many nations, many faiths. The Arabic culture was . . . and to some extent still is, a bridge, the main bridge between East and West . . .

Sami had also used a quotation from Professor Briffault's *Making of Humanity*. It read:

Science is the most momentous contribution of Arab civilization to the modern world. For although there is not a single aspect of European growth in which the decisive influence of Islamic culture is not traceable, nowhere is it so clear and momentous as in the genesis of that power which constitutes the permanent distinctive force of the modern world, and the supreme source of its victory—natural science and the scientific spirit.

Now that Sami was an American citizen, married, with three children, did he expect his family to follow the religion of Islam?

"My wife is a Catholic," Sami told me, "and she is raising the children as Catholics. As for me, I shall continue to be a Moslem. Both Christianity and Islam, as contrasting expressions of the same great truths, have much to offer humanity, I feel, but since I was raised a Moslem, I prefer to stay one."

Sami pointed to another quotation in Landau's book and said, "This description of Islam has always meant a lot to me in trying to explain my religion to Americans." I read the following:

> The ideal of the Moslem must needs reflect universalism —a comprehension of the universe which embraces not only man and nature but even God, the heavens and eternity. Thus the *finite* concerns them less than the *infinite*. . . . The Moslems who believed that God reveals Himself in the world at every moment of existence and that this world is constantly being created by Him, regarded the universe not as finite, not as being, but as becoming.

It was difficult for me at times to realize that this slender, dark American in front of me had been a Bedouin, a shepherd on the desert of Arabia not too many years before, and now he was telling me how Islam had sustained Arabs through centuries of poverty and misery.

"After the once great Arab culture you can imagine how the Arabs felt when they lived under the Turks as hewers of wood and carriers of water," Sami said to me. "But I believe they have been able to endure through the years because Islam has kept alive their hopes of a better tomorrow."

I asked Sami if he had ever encountered trouble from hecklers in his audience when he discussed the Arab world.

"Once or twice I have had someone try to convince my audiences that I didn't know what I was talking about," he said with a smile. "But it is difficult to find trouble when one looks only for good. I love this country, and my only reason for discussing the Arabs is to try to promote better understanding."

If it had not been for Sami's wife that night, I probably would never have known the story of young Nasry, a Palestinian refugee boy. Sami and his wife had "adopted" Nasry through an American orphanage in Bethlehem, Jordan. Although they could not bring him to America, they supported him through their voluntary payments. Nasry's parents had been killed in the Arab-Israeli war.

"He is a fine young man," Sami told me proudly. "He has learned to read and write English, and you should see some of the letters he has written us."

Sami's wife insisted that he show me a recent letter. I found it unusually clear for a fourteen-year-old boy:

We study in school about America. I learn you fight for freedom and found your great America in 1776. Some older Arabs tell me you fight for freedom and self-respect, same as Arabs fight today for theirs. They say some day Arab people will be one people with one flag like America. Is this bad?

One night I hear two Arab men talk about communism. One says it is good, the other says it is bad. When one man says communism does not allow belief in Allah, then I know communism must be bad, for how can anyone live without praying to Allah? I hear much on radio here about Americans with dark color skins being given different treatment from Americans with white skins. Is this true? I like to believe, as you told me, that America is land of freedom for everyone, even someday for me. I cannot thank you enough for giving me opportunity here to learn more about my own people as well as other people in the world.

I knew that Sami was embarrassed to have me read this exchange of correspondence, but I convinced him it would be helpful to me in writing this book. It would help Americans to understand the Arabs better, especially an Arab who had left the desert to become an American. This was Sami's reply to Nasry in Bethlehem:

Let me try to answer your questions about America. I know you hear much Russian propaganda on the radio. I shall tell you the truth as I know it. It is true that some Americans do not want to become friends with our American Negroes. But let me assure you, Nasry, the great majority of Americans have no prejudice against anyone because of the color of their skin, or because of their religion. My skin is dark, my religion is the same as yours, but I have freedom in America. And almost all Americans believe in this freedom which this country has fought for in two world wars.

Communists spend much time and money to picture Americans as money-mad, materially minded people. But they do not show the true side of America to the world. This greatness comes not from material resources alone, or military forces, but from those things we do not feel or touch. It comes from the American spirit, not from armies, ships, planes and tanks, but from churches, temples, universities, from unselfish and dedicated American men and women who believe in America and in the rights of all men. There is much for you to learn about America, Nasry, and there is much for Americans to learn about the Arabs. There is a great need for understanding, for knowing each other better. Only through this understanding can we attain peace.

In one of our great buildings in New York City, the architect has inscribed these words upon the walls: "Man's ultimate destiny depends not upon whether he can learn new lessons or make new discoveries and conquests, but on his acceptance of the lessons taught him 2000 years ago."

Those lessons, Nasry, are for all of us, I believe. They include understanding, tolerance, brotherly love, good will and the recognition that all men everywhere are the sons of God, or Allah. The American national motto is, "In God We Trust." Your motto is basically the same: "In Allah We Trust." If we all hold fast to these beliefs, we can know that the future will be bright with hope, filled with progress for your people and mine. May Allah and God, one and the same, give all mankind the love and understanding which we all need.

Sami drove me into New York City that night to Idlewild Airport to catch my plane for Los Angeles. I asked him one last question as I left him. "What made you work so hard to become an American?"

"I wanted to be an example of how a Saudi Arab could improve himself," he told me. "Aramco taught me to dress in a clean shirt and pants. I wanted to prove I had a right to wear them."

I have thought often of Sami Hussein's statement since that night in New York. There was a spirit of dignity in that answer, the same spirit of dignity which I believe prevails in the Arab countries today and will aid in solving the difficult problems that face this important and challenging area of the world.

Epilogue

As I have written the previous chapters of this book, I have wished I had the knowledge to write about both Arabs and Israelis. As an American who went to work in the Middle East, I have written only about the Arabs, since it was the Arabs I learned to know from firsthand observation.

There have been many excellent books written about Israel and Zionism. Among those recommended by the American Zionist Council are these: *Fulfillment* by Rufus Learsi (World Publishing Company, 1951), *Israel Today* by Ruth Gruber (Hill & Wang, 1958), *Politics of Israel* by Marver Bernstein (Princeton University Press, 1957), and *The Birth of Israel* by Garcia Granados (Alfred A. Knopf, 1948).

Each of these books I found interesting and challenging reading. I do not agree with all points of view advanced, but strongly as I may disagree I would always recommend that the Israeli case be read, heard, and debated by as many people as possible. It is only when a point of view is suppressed that truth becomes endangered.

In my lectures on the Middle East I have stressed the magnificent rebuilding job undertaken by the Israelis. No one could visit Israel without being impressed by the visible manifestation of progress, the courage of the Jewish people coming from every corner of the earth to reclaim barren land, plant forests, and build cities and towns. But is not the attitude of the Israeli government and its people toward the Arabs just as important as the progress?

Recently Prime Minister Ben Gurion of Israel said to an American newspaperman:

In 10 years I have had no direct contact with the Arabs. Before that I had contact with simple Arabs as I worked in the fields. I met others in the Turkish University. And as Chairman of the Jewish Agency I dealt with many. *I don't know what their thinking is now.*

Would Ben Gurion's last sentence be the key, perhaps, to Arab-Israeli relations? Could it be the reason so many Israelis consider the Arabs backward, fanatical, illiterate? How can a person truly assess his neighbor when he has no contact with him and tends to ridicule him at the slightest provocation? Is not this contact with the Arabs vitally necessary to the preservation of Israel?

Dr. Albert Einstein, the renowned scientist, once broadcast to Zionists in Europe this message:

> It is important to reach an understanding with the Arabs: to do this is the responsibility—not of the Arabs, not of the British, but of the Jews. And to reach such understanding is not less important than the founding of new institutions in Palestine.

The Israelis can render an invaluable service to their cause by upgrading their concept of the Arabs, by seeing them as their equals, recognizing them as their fellowmen to be respected and loved. Judaism stresses the brotherhood of man. Israel, which has been given so much from the rich storehouse, both material and spiritual, of Jews all over the world, surely can offer sincere, constructive suggestions for the settlement of the Arab refugee problem.

Intelligent Arabs do not want Israel destroyed. Nor do intelligent Israelis want the Arab refugee problem unsolved, a pitiful reminder of man's inhumanity to man. Two great Semitic peoples, the Jews and Arabs, have much to offer each other if only the bitterness and hatred can be lessened.

Several years ago, during a tour of the Arab states, I came across a heart-warming incident. It involved a poor Arab farmer, his wife, and a Jewish merchant. Because of the compassion and love of his fellowman, the Jew made it possible for the Arab to give a gift to his wife, a golden shawl, worth many times what the Arab paid for it.

The incident itself was probably unimportant, except for the joy it brought the Arab and his wife. It was a simple event, but it had deep human values attached to it. I have often remembered it when confronted by people who say the situation in the Middle East is hopeless. I do not believe this is true. The situation can never be hopeless as long as there is the spark of human kindness alive in the hearts of thousands of Israelis and Arabs.

The panorama which unfolds today in the Middle East, I believe, is one of hope, not defeat, of challenge, not accomplishment alone. It is a slowly developing picture in which man reaches out for his freedom, his individuality, his God-given rights. Nothing can prevent *this* picture from coming into full focus.

Selected Bibliography

Arab Unity: Hope and Fulfillment, Fayez A. Sayegh. New York: Devin-Adair Co., 1958

Arabian Jubilee, H. St.J. B. Philby. London: Robert Hale, Ltd., 1952

Arab of the Desert, H. R. P. Dickson. London: George Allen & Unwin, Ltd., 1949

Arab World: Past, Present and Future, Nejla Izzeddin. Chicago: Henry Regnery Co., 1953

Arabs, Oil and History, Kermit Roosevelt. New York: Harper & Bros., 1949

Arab Refugee Problem, Joseph Schechtman. New York: Philosophical Library, Inc., 1952

Arab Contribution to Civilization, Rom Landau. San Francisco: American Academy of Asian Studies, 1958

Heritage of the Desert, Harry B. Ellis. New York: Ronald Press Co., 1956

Doubts and Dynamite: The Middle East Today, Emile Bustani. London: Allan Wingate, 1958

Judaism or Jewish Nationalism, Elmer Berger. New York: Bookman Associates, Inc., 1957

Lawrence of Arabia, Richard Aldington. Chicago: Henry Regnery Co., 1955

Lord of Arabia, Ibn Saud, H. C. Armstrong. Beirut, Lebanon: Khayat's College Book Cooperative, 1954

Moslems on the March, F. W. Fernau. New York: Alfred A. Knopf, Inc., 1954

Mohammedanism, an Historical Survey, H. A. R. Gibb, London: Oxford University Press, 1953

History of the Arabs, Philip K. Hitti. New York: The Macmillan Co., 1952

Suleiman the Magnificent, Harold Lamb. Garden City, New York: Doubleday & Co., 1951

Saudi Arabia, Karl S. Twitchell. Princeton, N. J.: Princeton University Press, 1958

There Goes the Middle East, Alfred M. Lilienthal. New York: Devin-Adair Co., 1957

Violent Truce: A Military Observer Looks at the Arab-Israeli Conflict, 1951-1955, Commander E. H. Hutchinson, USNR. New York: Devin-Adair Co., 1958

Will the Middle East Go West?, Freda Utley. Chicago: Henry Regnery Co., 1957

PERIODICALS:

The author has found the following American newspapers and periodicals of much help: *The Christian Science Monitor, The Los Angeles Times, The Middle East Journal, Lands East, The Jewish Newsletter, Aramco World.*

Foreign publications of value have included: *The Middle East Forum, The London Sunday Times, The Manchester Guardian, Dhahran Sun and Flare.*

About the Author

Grant C. Butler began his writing career as a sports reporter on the Chicago *Herald-American* in 1939. During World War II he was a combat radio reporter for the Ninth Air Force in Europe. He worked in Saudi Arabia from 1948 to 1951, where he headed the Field Public Relations Division for ARAMCO. He has traveled extensively in the Arab countries, and his articles and short stories on the Middle East have appeared in national magazines and newspapers. He has given over a thousand lectures and earned several awards for contributing to "better American-Arab understanding." He is presently Director of Public Relations for the Associated Piping & Engineering Company of Los Angeles and Gulfport, Mississippi.

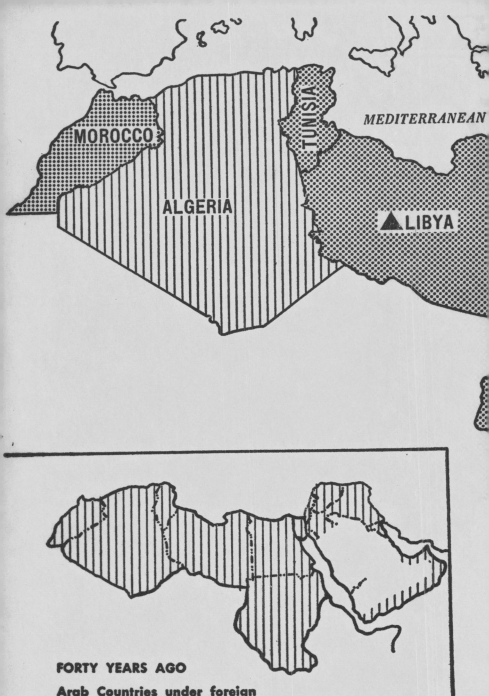

MEDITERRANEAN

MOROCCO

ALGERIA

TUNISIA

▲LIBYA

FORTY YEARS AGO

Arab Countries under foreign
mandate or protectorate, or
occupied by foreign troops.